Navigating the Digital Frontier

Cyber Security Manager's Handbook

SUDHEER KUMAR

First Edition 2024 Published by Sudheer Kumar

© 2024 by Sudheer Kumar.

All rights reserved.

No part of this book may be reproduced or utilized in any form or by any means, electronic or mechanical, including photocopying, recording, or by any information storage and retrieval system, without permission in writing from the publisher.

ISBN: 9798324256593

CONTENTS

Chapter 1: Introduction to Cyber Security Management
- Understanding the Role of a Cyber Security Manager
- Overview of Cyber Threat Landscape
- Importance of Effective Cyber Security Management

Chapter 2: Building a Cyber Security Team
- Identifying Key Roles and Responsibilities
- Recruiting and Hiring Talented Professionals
- Fostering a Collaborative and Innovative Team Culture

Chapter 3: Developing a Cyber Security Strategy
- Conducting Risk Assessments and Threat Modeling
- Establishing Clear Objectives and Goals
- Aligning Cyber Security Strategy with Business Objectives

Chapter 4: Implementing Security Policies and Procedures
- Creating Comprehensive Security Policies
- Establishing Incident Response Plans
- Conducting Regular Security Audits and Assessments

Chapter 5: Securing Networks and Infrastructure
- Implementing Firewalls, Intrusion Detection Systems and Intrusion Prevention Systems
- Protecting Data with Encryption and Access Controls
- Securing Cloud Infrastructure and Services

Chapter 6: Managing Identity and Access

- *Implementing Multi-Factor Authentication*
- *Managing User Access Privileges and Roles*
- *Securing Third-Party Access and Vendor Relationships*

Chapter 7: Monitoring and Incident Response

- Establishing Security Monitoring and Alerting Systems
- Responding to Security Incidents and Breaches
- Conducting Post-Incident Analysis and Remediation

Chapter 8: Compliance and Regulatory Requirements

- *Understanding Legal and Regulatory Frameworks*
- *Ensuring Compliance with Industry Standards*
- *Navigating International Data Protection Regulations*

Chapter 9: Cyber Security Training and Awareness

- *Educating Employees on Security Best Practices*
- *Conducting Regular Security Awareness Training*
- *Creating a Culture of Security Awareness and Responsibility*

Chapter 10: Emerging Technologies and Trends

- *Exploring Artificial Intelligence and Machine Learning in Cyber Security*
- *Addressing IoT Security Challenges*
- *Navigating the Risks and Opportunities of Blockchain Technology*

Chapter 11: Cyber Security Governance and Leadership

- *Engaging with Executive Leadership and Board of Directors*
- *Communicating the Value of Cyber Security Investments*
- *Building Trust and Credibility as a Cyber Security Leader*

Chapter 12: Future-Outlook and Continuous Improvement
- *Anticipating Future Threats and Challenges*
- *Embracing a Culture of Continuous Improvement*
- *Leading Innovation in Cyber Security Management*

Conclusion: The Journey Ahead
- *Reflecting on the Evolution of Cyber Security Management*
- *Empowering Cyber Security Managers to Lead with Confidence*
- *Embracing the Opportunities and Challenges of Securing the Digital Frontier*

Appendix: Resources for Cyber Security Managers
- *Recommended Reading List*
- *Online Training and Certification Programs*
- *Professional Organizations and Networking Opportunities*

About the Author:

Chapter 1

Introduction to Cyber Security Management

In an increasingly interconnected world, where digital technologies pervade every aspect of our lives, the importance of cyber security cannot be overstated.

From protecting sensitive data to safeguarding critical infrastructure, the role of cyber security management has become paramount in ensuring the safety and security of individuals, organizations, and nations alike.

Cyber security management encompasses a wide range of activities aimed at protecting digital assets, mitigating cyber threats, and ensuring the resilience of information systems. It involves strategic planning, risk management, policy development, and operational oversight to address the ever-evolving landscape of cyber threats.

At its core, cyber security management is about balancing the need for accessibility and usability with the imperative of confidentiality, integrity, and availability of data. It requires a holistic approach that integrates technical solutions, human factors, and organizational processes to create a robust security posture.

Key Components of Cyber Security Management

Risk Assessment and Management: Cyber security management begins with understanding the risks facing an organization's digital assets. This involves identifying potential threats, assessing vulnerabilities, and evaluating the potential impact of security incidents. Risk management strategies, such as risk mitigation, risk transfer, and risk acceptance, are then employed to minimize the organization's exposure to cyber threats.

Security Policy Development:
Establishing comprehensive security policies and procedures is essential for guiding organizational behavior and enforcing security controls.

These policies outline the acceptable use of digital resources, define roles and responsibilities for security personnel, and establish guidelines for incident response and recovery.

Security Architecture and Infrastructure: Implementing robust security architecture and infrastructure is critical for protecting digital assets from cyber threats.

This includes deploying firewalls, intrusion detection systems, encryption technologies, and access controls to safeguard networks, systems, and data.

Security Awareness and Training: Educating employees about cyber security best practices is fundamental for creating a culture of security awareness and responsibility within an organization. Training programs should cover topics such as password hygiene, phishing awareness, and social engineering tactics to empower employees to recognize and respond to security threats effectively.

Incident Response and Recovery:

Despite best efforts to prevent security incidents, organizations must be prepared to respond swiftly and effectively when breaches occur.

Establishing an incident response plan, conducting regular drills and exercises, and maintaining backups of critical data are essential components of a comprehensive incident response and recovery strategy.

Compliance and Regulatory Requirements: Compliance with industry regulations and legal requirements is a key consideration for cyber security management. Organizations must ensure that they adhere to relevant data protection laws, industry standards, and regulatory frameworks to avoid legal liabilities and reputational damage.

Understanding the Role of a Cyber Security Manager

In today's digital age, where cyber threats loom large and data breaches are a constant concern, the role of a cyber security manager is more critical than ever before. A cyber security manager plays a pivotal role in safeguarding an organization's digital assets, protecting against cyber threats, and ensuring the integrity and confidentiality of sensitive information. Let's delve deeper into the key responsibilities and duties of a cyber security manager:

Key Responsibilites of Cyber Security Manager

Strategic Planning and Management	Policy Development and Enforcement	Security Architecture and Infrastructure	Incident Response and Recovery	Compliance and Regulatory Compliance	Security Awareness and Training

Strategic Planning and Risk Management:

A cyber security manager is responsible for developing and implementing strategic plans to mitigate cyber risks and protect the organization's digital infrastructure.

This involves conducting comprehensive risk assessments, identifying potential vulnerabilities, and evaluating the potential impact of security incidents.

Based on these assessments, the cyber security manager develops risk management strategies and implements controls to minimize the organization's exposure to cyber threats.

Cyber Security Manager's Handbook

Policy Development and Enforcement:

A cyber security manager is tasked with developing, implementing, and enforcing security policies and procedures across the organization.

These policies outline the acceptable use of digital resources, define roles and responsibilities for security personnel, and establish guidelines for incident response and recovery.

By enforcing security policies, the cyber security manager helps create a culture of security awareness and responsibility within the organization.

Security Architecture and Infrastructure:

The cyber security manager is responsible for designing and implementing robust security architecture and infrastructure to protect against cyber threats.

This includes deploying firewalls, intrusion detection systems, encryption technologies, and access controls to safeguard networks, systems, and data.

The cyber security manager also ensures that security measures are integrated seamlessly into the organization's IT infrastructure and operations.

Incident Response and Recovery:

Despite best efforts to prevent security incidents, organizations may still experience breaches or cyber-attacks.

Cyber security manager is responsible for developing and implementing an incident response plan to address security incidents in a timely and effective manner.

This involves coordinating with internal teams, external partners, and law enforcement agencies to contain the incident, investigate the root cause, and mitigate the impact on the organization's operations and reputation.

Security Awareness and Training:

Educating employees about cyber security best practices is a critical aspect of the cyber security manager's role.

The cyber security manager develops and delivers training programs to raise awareness about common cyber threats, such as phishing attacks, malware infections, and social engineering tactics.

By empowering employees to recognize and respond to security threats effectively, the cyber security manager helps strengthen the organization's overall security posture.

Compliance and Regulatory Compliance:

Ensuring compliance with industry regulations and legal requirements is a key responsibility of the cyber security manager.

The cyber security manager must stay abreast of relevant data protection laws, industry standards, and regulatory frameworks and ensure that the organization adheres to these requirements.

This may involve conducting regular audits and assessments, maintaining documentation of security measures, and reporting on compliance status to executive leadership and regulatory authorities.

In conclusion, the role of a cyber security manager is multifaceted and requires a combination of technical expertise, strategic thinking, and strong leadership skills.

By effectively managing cyber risks, implementing robust security measures, and fostering a culture of security awareness, the cyber security manager plays a crucial role in protecting the organization's digital assets and reputation in an increasingly complex and interconnected world.

Overview of Cyber Threat Landscape

In today's interconnected digital world, the cyber threat landscape is vast, complex, and constantly evolving. Cyber threats pose significant risks to individuals, organizations, governments, and society. Understanding the diverse range of cyber threats is essential for developing effective cyber security strategies and mitigating potential risks. Let us explore some of the key elements of the cyber threat landscape:

Malware:

Malware, short for malicious software, is a broad category of software designed to disrupt, damage, or gain unauthorized access to computer systems and networks.

Types of malwares include viruses, worms, trojans, ransomware, spyware, and adware etc.

Malware can be spread through email attachments, malicious websites, infected USB drives, and other vectors.

Phishing and Social Engineering:

Phishing is a cyber-attack method in which attackers use deceptive emails, websites, or messages to trick individuals into revealing sensitive information, such as passwords, credit card numbers, or personal data.

Social engineering involves manipulating people into performing actions, confidential information through psychological manipulation or deceit.

Distributed Denial of Service (DDoS) Attacks:

DDoS attacks involve flooding a target system or network with a large volume of traffic or requests, rendering it inaccessible to legitimate users.

DDoS attacks can disrupt services, cause financial losses, and damage the reputation of targeted organizations.

Insider Threats:

Insider threats refer to security risks posed by individuals within an organization, such as employees, contractors, or partners, who misuse their access privileges or intentionally disclose sensitive information.

Insider threats can result from negligence, malicious intent, or coercion.

Advanced Persistent Threats (APTs):

APTs are sophisticated and stealthy cyber-attacks launched by well-funded and highly skilled adversaries, such as nation-state actors or organized cybercrime groups.

APTs typically involve targeted attacks against specific organizations or individuals over an extended period, with the goal of stealing sensitive information or disrupting operations.

Data Breaches:

Data breaches involve unauthorized access to sensitive data, such as personal information, financial records, or intellectual property.

Sudheer Kumar

Data breaches can have severe consequences, including financial losses, regulatory penalties, legal liabilities, and reputational damage.

Supply Chain Attacks:

Supply chain attacks target vulnerabilities in the software supply chain to compromise trusted software or hardware components used by organizations.

Attackers may infiltrate software vendors, distributors, or third-party suppliers to insert malicious code or compromise legitimate updates.

Internet of Things (IoT) Vulnerabilities:

IoT devices, such as smart appliances, wearable devices, and industrial sensors, are vulnerable to cyber-attacks due to insecure configurations, lack of security updates, and limited processing power.

Compromised IoT devices can be used to launch large-scale botnet attacks or gain unauthorized access to networks.

Zero-Day Exploits:

Zero-day exploits are vulnerabilities in software or hardware that are not publicly known and for which no patch or fix is available.

Attackers exploit zero-day vulnerabilities to launch targeted attacks before security patches can be developed and deployed.

Cyber Espionage and Warfare:

Cyber espionage involves the theft of sensitive information or intellectual property for political, economic, or military purposes.

Cyber warfare encompasses offensive cyber operations conducted by nation-states or state-sponsored actors to disrupt or disable critical infrastructure, government systems, or military networks.

In conclusion, the cyber threat landscape is dynamic and constantly evolving, with adversaries employing increasingly sophisticated tactics, techniques, and procedures to exploit vulnerabilities and achieve their objectives. Addressing these threats requires a multi-layered approach, combining technical controls, security awareness training, threat intelligence, and collaboration among stakeholders to effectively mitigate risks and protect against cyber-attacks.

Sudheer Kumar

Importance of Effective Cyber Security Management

In an increasingly digital world where businesses, governments, and individuals rely heavily on technology for everyday operations, effective cyber security management has become more crucial than ever before. Here are some key reasons why effective cyber security management is of paramount importance:

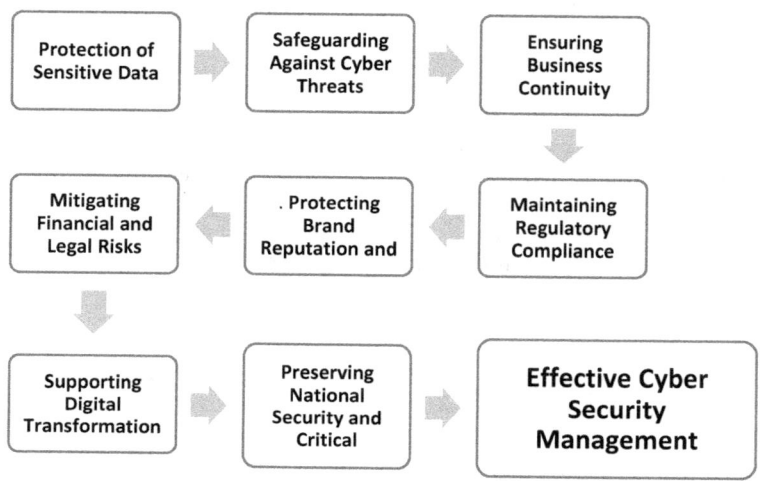

Protection of Sensitive Data:

Effective cyber security management ensures the protection of sensitive data, including personal information, financial records, intellectual property, and proprietary business data.

Data breaches can result in severe financial losses, regulatory penalties, legal liabilities, and reputational damage for organizations.

Safeguarding Against Cyber Threats:

Cyber threats, such as malware, phishing attacks, ransomware, and DDoS attacks, pose significant risks to organizations' digital assets and operations.

Effective cyber security management helps organizations detect, prevent, and respond to cyber threats in a timely and effective manner, minimizing the impact of security incidents.

Sudheer Kumar

Ensuring Business Continuity:

Cyber security incidents, such as data breaches or network outages, can disrupt business operations, leading to downtime, lost productivity, and revenue losses.

By implementing robust cyber security measures and incident response plans, organizations can mitigate the risk of disruptions and ensure business continuity even in the face of cyber-attacks.

Maintaining Regulatory Compliance:

Many industries are subject to regulatory requirements and compliance mandates related to data protection, privacy, and information security.

Effective cyber security management helps organizations comply with regulatory standards, such as GDPR, HIPAA, PCI DSS, and SOX, avoiding fines, penalties, and legal sanctions.

Protecting Brand Reputation and Customer Trust:

A data breach or security incident can have a significant impact on an organization's brand reputation and customer trust.

Effective cyber security management demonstrates a commitment to protecting customer data and privacy, enhancing brand reputation, and building trust with stakeholders.

Mitigating Financial and Legal Risks:

Cyber security incidents can result in significant financial losses due to remediation costs, legal fees, regulatory fines, and litigation expenses.

Effective cyber security management helps organizations mitigate financial and legal risks associated with security breaches, reducing the potential impact on the bottom line.

Supporting Digital Transformation and Innovation:

Cyber security is an enabler of digital transformation and innovation, allowing organizations to embrace new technologies and business models with confidence.

Effective cyber security management enables organizations to securely leverage cloud computing, IoT, AI, and other emerging technologies to drive innovation and competitive advantage.

Preserving National Security and Critical Infrastructure:

Cyber-attacks targeting critical infrastructure, government systems, and national security assets pose a significant threat to public safety, economic stability, and national security.

Effective cyber security management is essential for protecting critical infrastructure and ensuring the resilience of national security systems against cyber threats.

In conclusion, effective cyber security management is essential for protecting organizations, individuals, and society from cyber threats, ensuring data privacy and security, maintaining regulatory compliance, preserving brand reputation and customer trust, mitigating financial and legal risks, supporting digital transformation and innovation, and safeguarding national security and critical infrastructure. By investing in robust cyber security measures and practices, organizations can mitigate cyber risks and build a secure and resilient digital ecosystem.

Chapter 2

Building a Cyber Security Team

Building a strong and effective cyber security team is essential for protecting organizations from cyber threats, mitigating risks, and ensuring the security of digital assets. A well-rounded cyber security team comprises individuals with diverse skills, expertise, and experience who work collaboratively to address the evolving threat landscape. Here is an overview of the key components involved in building a cyber security team:

Identify Key Roles and Responsibilities:

As a cyber security manager, one of your primary responsibilities is to build and lead a team capable of protecting the organization's digital assets and mitigating cyber risks effectively. Identifying key roles and responsibilities within your cyber security team is crucial for ensuring that all aspects of the organization's security posture are adequately addressed. Here is an overview of the key roles and responsibilities to consider:

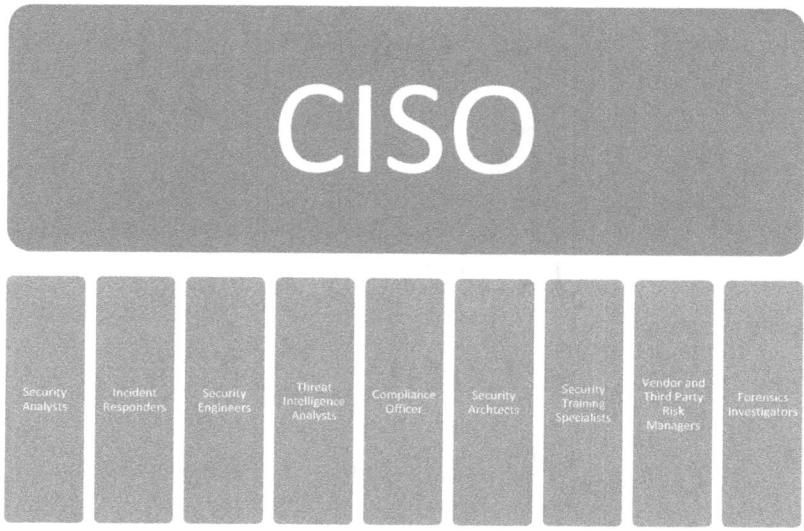

Chief Information Security Officer (CISO):

The CISO is the senior executive responsible for overseeing the organization's overall cyber security strategy and operations.

Responsibilities include developing and implementing security policies and procedures, managing the cyber security budget, and providing strategic guidance to senior leadership.

Security Analysts:

Security analysts are responsible for monitoring and analysing security alerts and events to detect and respond to cyber threats.

Responsibilities include conducting threat assessments, investigating security incidents, and providing recommendations for improving the organization's security posture.

Sudheer Kumar

Incident Responders:

Incident responders are responsible for managing and coordinating the response to security incidents, such as data breaches, malware infections, or DDoS attacks.

Responsibilities include containing the incident, conducting forensics investigations, and implementing remediation measures to minimize the impact on the organization.

Security Engineers:

Security engineers are responsible for designing, implementing, and maintaining security controls and infrastructure to protect the organization's networks, systems, and data.

Responsibilities include configuring firewalls, intrusion detection systems, encryption technologies, and access controls to mitigate cyber risks.

Threat Intelligence Analysts:

Threat intelligence analysts are responsible for monitoring and analyzing cyber threats and trends to identify emerging threats and vulnerabilities.

Responsibilities include gathering intelligence from open-source intelligence (OSINT), dark web forums, and threat feeds, and providing actionable insights to the cyber security team.

Compliance Officers:

Compliance officers are responsible for ensuring that the organization complies with relevant regulatory requirements and industry standards related to cyber security.

Compliance officers conducting compliance assessments, maintaining documentation of security measures, and reporting on compliance status to regulatory authorities.

Security Architects:

Security architects are responsible for designing and implementing security architecture and infrastructure to protect against cyber threats.

Responsibilities include designing secure networks, systems, and applications, and ensuring that security measures are integrated seamlessly into the organization's IT infrastructure.

Security Awareness and Training Specialists:

Security awareness and training specialists are responsible for educating employees about cyber security best practices and promoting a culture of security awareness within the organization.

Responsibilities include developing and delivering training programs, conducting phishing simulations, and providing guidance on security policies and procedures.

Vendor and Third-Party Risk Managers:

Vendor and third-party risk managers are responsible for assessing and managing cyber risks associated with third-party vendors, suppliers, and partners.

Responsibilities include conducting risk assessments, reviewing vendor contracts, and implementing controls to mitigate third-party cyber risks.

Forensics Investigators:

Forensics investigators are responsible for conducting digital forensics investigations to identify the root cause of security incidents and gather evidence for legal or regulatory purposes.

Responsibilities include collecting and analyzing digital evidence, preserving chain of custody, and preparing reports for law enforcement or internal stakeholders.

In conclusion, identifying key roles and responsibilities within your cyber security team is essential for building a comprehensive and effective security program. By defining clear roles and responsibilities, allocating resources effectively, and fostering collaboration among team members, you can strengthen your organization's security posture and effectively mitigate cyber risks.

Sudheer Kumar

Recruiting and Hiring Talented Professionals

As a cyber security manager, building a skilled and effective team is essential for protecting your organization against cyber threats and ensuring the security of its digital assets. Recruiting and hiring talented professionals with the right skills, expertise, and mindset is critical to the success of your cyber security program. Here is an overview of the approach you can take to recruit and hire talented professionals:

Define Job Roles and Requirements:

Start by clearly defining the job roles and responsibilities for each position within your cyber security team. Identify the specific skills, qualifications, certifications, and experience required for each role, considering the organization's cyber security needs and priorities.

Develop Compelling Job Descriptions:

Craft compelling and detailed job descriptions that accurately reflect the responsibilities, requirements, and expectations for each position.

Highlight the organization's mission, culture, and values to attract candidates who align with its goals and ethos. Emphasize opportunities for growth, learning, and advancement within the cyber security team to attract top talent.

Utilize Multiple Recruitment Channels:

Cast a wide net and utilize multiple recruitment channels to attract talented professionals, including job boards, professional networking sites, social media platforms, and industry-specific forums.

Leverage personal and professional networks, referrals, and recommendations from colleagues and industry contacts to identify potential candidates.

Screen and Evaluate Candidates:

Develop a structured screening and evaluation process to assess candidates' skills, qualifications, and suitability for the role.

Review resumes, portfolios, and credentials to identify candidates who meet the job requirements and possess relevant experience and expertise.

Conduct preliminary phone or video interviews to assess candidates' communication skills, technical proficiency, and cultural fit with the organization.

Conduct In-Depth Interviews:

Invite promising candidates for in-depth interviews to assess their technical skills, problem-solving abilities, and alignment with the organization's values and culture.

Ask targeted questions to evaluate candidates' experience, expertise, and approach to cyber security challenges.

Conduct behavioural interviews to assess candidates' soft skills, such as teamwork, communication, and adaptability.

Assess Cultural Fit and Alignment:

Evaluate candidates' cultural fit and alignment with the organization's values, mission, and goals.

Consider factors such as work ethic, integrity, passion for cyber security, and willingness to learn and adapt to new challenges.

Look for candidates who demonstrate a commitment to continuous improvement, collaboration, and excellence in their work.

Provide Opportunities for Skills Assessment:

Offer candidates opportunities to demonstrate their technical skills and expertise through skills assessments, coding challenges, or practical exercises.

Assess candidates' problem-solving abilities, analytical thinking, and technical proficiency in relevant areas of cyber security.

Offer Competitive Compensation and Benefits:

Ensure that your organization offers competitive compensation packages and benefits to attract and retain top cyber security talent.

Consider factors such as salary, bonuses, health benefits, retirement plans, professional development opportunities, and work-life balance initiatives.

Provide Feedback and Follow-Up:

Provide timely feedback to candidates throughout the recruitment and hiring process, keeping them informed of their progress and status.

Offer constructive feedback to unsuccessful candidates, highlighting areas for improvement and encouraging them to apply for future opportunities.

Follow up with successful candidates to extend job offers, negotiate terms, and facilitate a smooth onboarding process.

Foster a Positive Candidate Experience:

Create a positive and memorable candidate experience that reflects positively on your organization and enhances its reputation as an employer of choice.

Communicate transparently, respectfully, and professionally with candidates at every stage of the recruitment process.

Provide a warm welcome to new hires and support them throughout their onboarding and integration into the cyber security team.

In conclusion, recruiting and hiring talented professionals as a cyber security manager requires careful planning, effective communication, and a commitment to excellence in every aspect of the hiring process. By following these steps and approaches, you can attract, evaluate, and onboard top cyber security talent to strengthen your organization's security posture and achieve its cyber security objectives.

Fostering a Collaborative and Innovative Team Culture

Fostering a collaborative and innovative team culture is essential for building a high-performing cyber security team that can effectively address the evolving threat landscape and protect the organization's digital assets. As a cyber security manager, you play a crucial role in creating an environment where team members feel empowered to collaborate, share ideas, and innovate to solve complex cyber security challenges. Here is an overview of the approach you can take to foster a collaborative and innovative cyber security team culture:

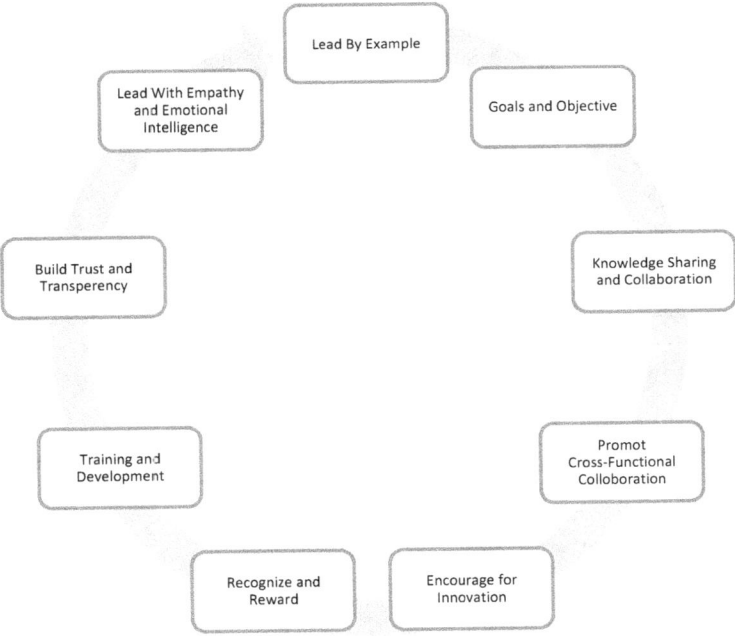

Lead by Example:

As a cyber security manager, led by example by demonstrating collaborative behaviours, open communication, and a commitment to innovation in your own work.

Encourage transparency, inclusivity, and accountability in all aspects of team interactions and decision-making processes.

Sudheer Kumar

Establish Shared Goals and Objectives:

Define clear and measurable goals and objectives for the cyber security team aligned with the organization's mission, vision, and strategic priorities.

Foster a shared sense of purpose and ownership among team members by involving them in the goal-setting process and soliciting their input and feedback.

Encourage Knowledge Sharing and Collaboration:

Create opportunities for knowledge sharing and collaboration among team members through regular meetings, brainstorming sessions, and collaborative projects.

Encourage team members to share insights, best practices, and lessons learned from their experiences to foster a culture of continuous learning and improvement.

Promote Cross-Functional Collaboration:

Facilitate collaboration and information sharing between the cyber security team and other departments, such as IT, legal, compliance, and risk management.

Foster a culture of cross-functional collaboration, where team members work closely with colleagues from different disciplines to address security challenges and achieve common goals.

Provide Opportunities for Innovation:

Create a supportive environment that encourages creativity, experimentation, and innovation in cyber security solutions and practices.

Provide opportunities for team members to explore new technologies, tools, and approaches to address emerging cyber threats and vulnerabilities.

Recognize and Reward Contributions:

Recognize and celebrate the achievements and contributions of individual team members and the team.

Provide meaningful recognition and rewards, such as praise, bonuses, promotions, or professional development opportunities, to acknowledge exceptional performance and foster a sense of accomplishment and motivation.

Foster a Culture of Continuous Improvement:

Encourage a culture of continuous improvement by soliciting feedback from team members, stakeholders, and external partners on processes, practices, and outcomes.

Use feedback and insights to identify opportunities for improvement and innovation, and take proactive steps to address challenges and enhance team performance.

Invest in Training and Development:
Invest in training and development programs to enhance the skills, knowledge, and capabilities of team members.

Provide opportunities for professional certifications, workshops, conferences, and specialized training courses to support the growth and advancement of team members in their careers.

Build Trust and Psychological Safety:

Foster an environment of trust, respect, and psychological safety where team members feel comfortable expressing their ideas, opinions, and concerns without fear of judgment or reprisal.

Create open channels of communication and encourage constructive feedback and dialogue to build strong relationships and foster collaboration within the team.

Lead with Empathy and Emotional Intelligence:

Lead with empathy and emotional intelligence by understanding and empathizing with the unique needs, perspectives, and experiences of team members.

Be approachable, supportive, and responsive to the needs and concerns of team members, and foster a culture of empathy, compassion, and support within the team.

In conclusion, fostering a collaborative and innovative cyber security team culture requires leadership, vision, and commitment from cyber security managers. By following these approaches and principles, you can create an environment where team members feel empowered to collaborate, share ideas, and innovate to address complex cyber security challenges effectively. Ultimately, fostering a collaborative and innovative team culture will strengthen your organization's security posture and resilience in the face of evolving cyber threat

Chapter 3

Developing a Cyber Security Strategy

Developing a robust cyber security strategy is essential for protecting your organization's digital assets, mitigating cyber risks, and ensuring resilience against cyber threats. As a cyber security manager, you play a crucial role in developing and implementing a comprehensive cyber security strategy that aligns with the organization's goals, objectives, and risk tolerance. Here is an overview of the approach you can take to develop a cyber security strategy:

Understand the Organization's Business Objectives:

Start by gaining a deep understanding of the organization's business objectives, mission, vision, and strategic priorities.

Identify key stakeholders and decision-makers who will be involved in shaping the cyber security strategy and aligning it with the organization's overall goals and objectives.

Conduct a Cyber Security Risk Assessment:

Conduct a comprehensive cyber security risk assessment to identify and prioritize cyber risks facing the organization. Evaluate the organization's assets, systems, networks, and data to identify vulnerabilities, threats, and potential impacts of security incidents.

Consider both internal and external factors, such as regulatory requirements, industry standards, emerging threats, and geopolitical risks, in the risk assessment process.

Define Cyber Security Goals and Objectives:

Based on the findings of the risk assessment, define clear and measurable cyber security goals and objectives that support the organization's business objectives.

Establish strategic priorities and focus areas for the cyber security strategy, such as data protection, threat detection and response, incident management, compliance, and resilience.

Develop a Cyber Security Framework and Roadmap:

Develop a cyber security framework and roadmap that outlines the strategic initiatives, projects, and actions needed to achieve the organization's cyber security goals and objectives.

Define key milestones, timelines, and resource requirements for implementing the cyber security strategy, considering budgetary constraints and organizational priorities.

Implement Security Controls and Measures:

Implement a range of security controls and measures to protect the organization's digital assets and mitigate cyber risks effectively.

Deploy technologies, such as firewalls, intrusion detection systems, encryption, and access controls, to safeguard networks, systems, and data.

Establish security policies, procedures, and guidelines to govern the acceptable use of digital resources and ensure compliance with regulatory requirements.

Foster a Culture of Security Awareness:

Foster a culture of security awareness and responsibility among employees by providing regular training, education, and awareness programs.

Raise awareness about common cyber threats, such as phishing, malware, social engineering, and password attacks, and empower employees to recognize and respond to security incidents effectively.

Establish Incident Response and Recovery Plans:

Develop and implement incident response and recovery plans to effectively detect, respond to, and recover from security incidents.

Define roles, responsibilities, and escalation procedures for responding to security incidents, and conduct regular drills and exercises to test the effectiveness of the plans.

Monitor, Measure, and Improve:

Implement mechanisms for monitoring, measuring, and reporting on the effectiveness of the cyber security strategy and its implementation.

Use key performance indicators (KPIs) and metrics to track progress, identify areas for improvement, and make data-driven decisions to enhance the organization's security posture.

Collaborate and Engage with Stakeholders:

Collaborate and engage with key stakeholders, including senior leadership, IT teams, legal, compliance, risk management, and external partners, to ensure alignment and support for the cyber security strategy.

Communicate regularly with stakeholders to provide updates on cyber security initiatives, share insights on emerging threats, and solicit feedback and input on cyber security matters.

Stay Agile and Adaptive:

Recognize that the cyber security landscape is constantly evolving, with new threats, vulnerabilities, and technologies emerging rapidly.

Stay agile and adaptive in your approach to cyber security, continuously monitoring industry trends, best practices, and regulatory requirements, and adapting your strategy and tactics accordingly.

In conclusion, developing a cyber security strategy requires a structured and proactive approach that considers the organization's business objectives, cyber risks, and regulatory requirements. By following these steps and principles, you can develop a robust cyber security strategy that effectively protects your organization's digital assets, mitigates cyber risks, and ensures resilience against cyber threats.

Conducting Risk Assessments and Threat Modeling

As a cyber security manager, conducting risk assessments and threat modeling is essential for identifying, prioritizing, and mitigating cyber risks that may impact your organization's digital assets and operations. Risk assessments and threat modeling provide valuable insights into potential vulnerabilities, threats, and impacts, enabling you to develop targeted mitigation strategies and allocate resources effectively. Here's an overview of the approach you can take for conducting risk assessments and threat modelling.

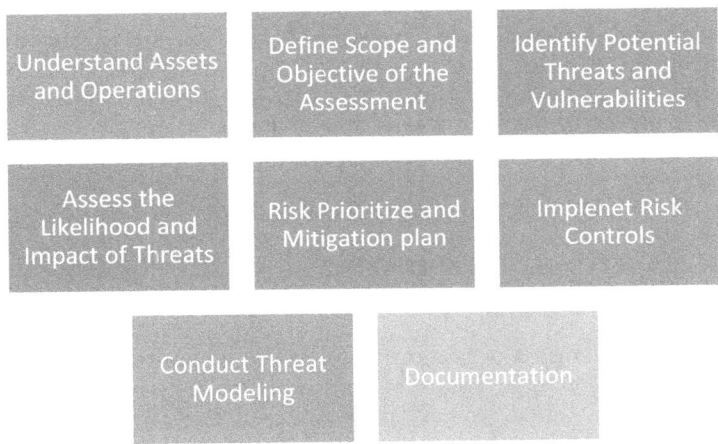

Understand the Organization's Assets and Operations:

Start by gaining a comprehensive understanding of the organization's assets, systems, networks, and operations.

Identify critical assets, such as sensitive data, intellectual property, infrastructure components, and key business processes, that may be at risk of cyber threats.

Define the Scope and Objectives of the Assessment:

Define the scope and objectives of the risk assessment and threat modeling exercise, including the assets and systems to be assessed, the threats to be considered, and the desired outcomes. Determine the methodology, tools, and resources needed to conduct the assessment effectively.

Identify Potential Threats and Vulnerabilities:

Identify potential threats and vulnerabilities that could exploit weaknesses in the organization's systems, networks, and applications.

Consider a range of threat actors, including hackers, insider threats, nation-state actors, and malicious insiders, and the tactics, techniques, and procedures (TTPs) they may employ.

Assess the Likelihood and Impact of Threats:

Assess the likelihood and impact of identified threats on the organization's assets, operations, and objectives. Use qualitative and quantitative methods to evaluate the probability of threats occurring and the potential consequences of security incidents, such as financial losses, reputational damage, and regulatory fines.

Prioritize Risks and Mitigation Measures:

Prioritize risks based on their likelihood, impact, and significance to the organization's business objectives and operations.

Develop a risk matrix or heat map to visualize and prioritize risks, and identify high-priority risks that require immediate attention and mitigation.

Develop Mitigation Strategies and Controls:

Develop targeted mitigation strategies and controls to address identified risks and vulnerabilities effectively.

Consider a range of preventive, detective, and corrective controls, such as access controls, encryption, intrusion detection systems, and incident response procedures, to mitigate cyber risks.

Implement Controls and Monitor Effectiveness:

Implement the identified controls and mitigation measures to reduce the organization's exposure to cyber risks.

Monitor the effectiveness of implemented controls through regular assessments, audits, and monitoring activities, and adjust as needed to address emerging threats and vulnerabilities.

Conduct Threat Modeling Exercises:

Conduct threat modeling exercises to systematically identify, analyse, and prioritize potential threats to the organization's assets and operations.

Use threat modeling techniques, such as attack trees, data flow diagrams, and threat matrices, to model potential attack scenarios and assess the likelihood and impact of threats.

Involve Stakeholders and Subject Matter Experts:

Involve key stakeholders, subject matter experts, and decision-makers from across the organization in the risk assessment and threat modeling process.

Foster collaboration and communication among stakeholders to ensure alignment, buy-in, and support for the risk mitigation strategies and controls.

Document Findings and Recommendations:

Document the findings, analysis, and recommendations from the risk assessment and threat modeling exercise in a comprehensive report.

Clearly communicate the identified risks, mitigation strategies, and action plans to senior leadership, IT teams, and other relevant stakeholders, and obtain approval and support for implementation.

In conclusion, conducting risk assessments and threat modeling is a critical aspect of effective cyber security management, enabling organizations to identify, prioritize, and mitigate cyber risks proactively. By following this approach and leveraging appropriate methodologies and tools, cyber security managers can gain valuable insights into potential threats and vulnerabilities, develop targeted mitigation strategies, and strengthen the organization's security posture against evolving cyber threats.

Sudheer Kumar

Establishing Clear Objectives and Goals

Establishing clear objectives and goals is fundamental to the success of any cyber security program. As a cyber security manager, it's essential to define specific, measurable, achievable, relevant, and time-bound (SMART) objectives that align with the organization's strategic priorities and support its overall mission. Here's an overview of the approach you can take to establish clear objectives and goals as a cyber security manager:

Understand Organizational Priorities:

Start by gaining a deep understanding of the organization's strategic priorities, business objectives, and risk tolerance.

Identify key stakeholders, including senior leadership, IT teams, legal, compliance, and risk management, who will be involved in shaping the cyber security objectives and goals.

Conduct a Cyber Security Assessment:

Conduct a comprehensive cyber security assessment to identify strengths, weaknesses, opportunities, and threats (SWOT) related to the organization's cyber security posture.

Evaluate the organization's current capabilities, resources, and processes to identify areas for improvement and alignment with industry best practices and standards.

Define Specific Objectives and Key Results (OKRs):

Define specific, measurable objectives and key results (OKRs) that align with the organization's strategic priorities and address its cyber security needs.

Ensure that objectives are SMART: specific, measurable, achievable, relevant, and time-bound, to provide clear direction and accountability for achieving results.

Prioritize Objectives Based on Risk and Impact:

Prioritize cyber security objectives based on the level of risk, potential impact, and significance to the organization's business objectives and operations.

Consider factors such as regulatory requirements, industry standards, emerging threats, and geopolitical risks when prioritizing objectives.

Establish Clear Metrics and KPIs:

Establish clear metrics and key performance indicators (KPIs) to measure progress and success in achieving cyber security objectives.

Define quantifiable measures of success, such as reduction in cyber incidents, improvement in incident response times, and compliance with regulatory requirements.

Align Objectives with Core Functions of Cyber Security:

Align cyber security objectives with the core functions of cyber security, including risk management, threat detection and response, access control, data protection, and compliance.

Ensure that objectives address key areas of vulnerability and exposure to cyber threats, such as network security, application security, and endpoint security.

Communicate Objectives and Gain Buy-In:

Clearly communicate cyber security objectives and goals to senior leadership, key stakeholders, and the cyber security team.

Gain buy-in and support from stakeholders by articulating the rationale, benefits, and expected outcomes of the cyber security objectives and their alignment with the organization's strategic priorities.

Develop Action Plans and Roadmaps:

Develop action plans and roadmaps to achieve cyber security objectives, outlining the specific steps, milestones, and timelines for implementation.

Identify resources, budgets, and dependencies needed to execute action plans effectively, and allocate responsibilities to team members accordingly.

Monitor Progress and Adapt as Needed:

Monitor progress towards achieving cyber security objectives and KPIs on an ongoing basis, using regular assessments, audits, and reporting mechanisms.

Adapt and adjust action plans as needed in response to changes in the threat landscape, emerging risks, and organizational priorities.

Celebrate Achievements and Continuous Improvement:

Celebrate achievements and milestones in achieving cyber security objectives, recognizing the contributions of team members and stakeholders.

Foster a culture of continuous improvement by soliciting feedback, identifying lessons learned, and incorporating best practices and insights into future objectives and goals.

In conclusion, establishing clear objectives and goals is essential for driving the success of a cyber security program and ensuring alignment with the organization's strategic priorities. By following this approach and leveraging SMART objectives, clear metrics, and effective communication strategies, cyber security managers can provide clear direction, accountability, and motivation for achieving cyber security excellence in their organizations.

Aligning Cyber Security Strategy with Business Objectives

Aligning cyber security strategy with business objectives is essential for ensuring that cyber security efforts effectively support and enable the organization's overall mission and strategic goals. As a cyber security manager, it's your responsibility to bridge the gap between cyber security and business priorities, ensuring that cyber security initiatives are closely aligned with the organization's strategic direction. Here's an overview of the approach you can take to align cyber security strategy with business objectives:

Understand Business Objectives:

Start by gaining a deep understanding of the organization's business objectives, mission, vision, and strategic priorities.

Engage with senior leadership, key stakeholders, and decision-makers to understand their goals, challenges, and expectations regarding cyber security.

Conduct a Business Impact Analysis:

Conduct a business impact analysis to identify and prioritize the critical business processes, functions, and assets that are essential for achieving the organization's objectives.

Assess the potential impact of cyber security incidents on these critical business assets and operations to quantify the business risk.

Identify Business-Critical Assets:

Identify and prioritize the organization's business-critical assets, such as sensitive data, intellectual property, customer information, and key infrastructure components.

Understand how these assets support the organization's strategic objectives and revenue-generating activities.

Align Cyber Security Objectives with Business Goals:

Align cyber security objectives and initiatives with the organization's business goals and strategic priorities.

Identify specific cyber security objectives that directly support and enable the achievement of business objectives, such as protecting customer data, ensuring business continuity, and maintaining regulatory compliance.

Establish Key Performance Indicators (KPIs):

Establish key performance indicators (KPIs) and metrics to measure the effectiveness of cyber security efforts in supporting business objectives.

Define quantifiable measures of success, such as reduction in cyber incidents, improvement in incident response times, and alignment with regulatory requirements.

Develop a Risk-Based Approach:

Develop a risk-based approach to cyber security that prioritizes resources and efforts based on the level of risk to critical business assets and operations.

Allocate resources and investments to cyber security initiatives that provide the greatest value and impact in mitigating business risks.

Foster Collaboration with Business Units:

Foster collaboration and communication with business units, departments, and functional areas to ensure that cyber security efforts are aligned with their specific needs and requirements.

Engage with business leaders and stakeholders to understand their cyber security concerns, priorities, and constraints, and incorporate their input into cyber security planning and decision-making.

Communicate the Business Value of Cyber Security:

Clearly communicate the business value of cyber security initiatives and investments to senior leadership, key stakeholders, and decision-makers.

Articulate the potential benefits of cyber security in terms of protecting business assets, safeguarding customer trust, enhancing brand reputation, and ensuring regulatory compliance.

Integrate Cyber Security into Business Processes:

Integrate cyber security considerations into key business processes, workflows, and decision-making processes.

Embed cyber security controls, policies, and procedures into business operations to ensure that cyber security becomes an integral part of the organization's culture and DNA.

Monitor Progress and Adapt as Needed:

Monitor progress towards achieving cyber security objectives and KPIs, and regularly assess the effectiveness of cyber security efforts in supporting business objectives.

Adapt and adjust cyber security strategies and initiatives as needed in response to changes in the business environment, emerging threats, and evolving regulatory requirements.

In conclusion, aligning cyber security strategy with business objectives requires a proactive and strategic approach that integrates cyber security into the organization's overall strategic planning and decision-making processes. By following this approach and fostering collaboration between cyber security and business units, cyber security managers can ensure that cyber security efforts are closely aligned with the organization's mission, vision, and strategic goals, ultimately enhancing the organization's resilience and competitiveness in an increasingly digital world.

Chapter 4

Implementing Security Policies and Procedures

Implementing security policies and procedures is essential for establishing a strong foundation of cyber security within an organization. As a cyber security manager, it is your responsibility to develop, implement, and enforce security policies and procedures that mitigate risks, protect sensitive information, and ensure compliance with relevant regulations and standards. Here is an overview of the approach you can take:

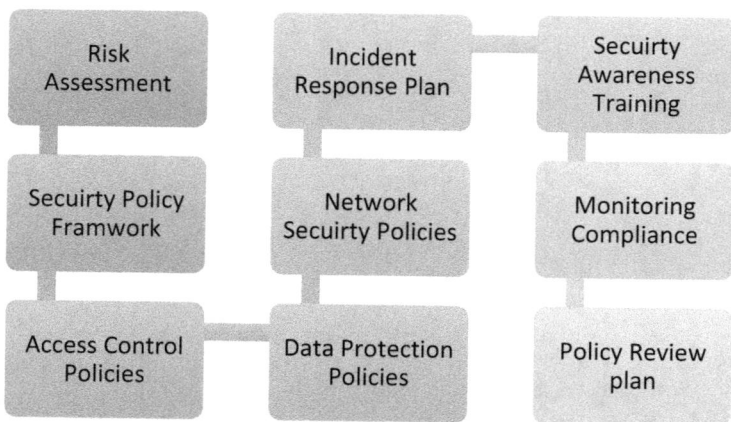

Cyber Security Manager's Handbook

Conduct a Comprehensive Risk Assessment:

Begin by conducting a thorough risk assessment to identify potential threats, vulnerabilities, and risks to the organization's assets, systems, and data.

Analyze the findings of the risk assessment to prioritize security measures and determine the areas where security policies and procedures are needed most urgently.

Define Security Policy Framework:

Develop a comprehensive security policy framework that outlines the organization's security objectives, principles, and guidelines.

Define the scope of the policies, including the types of information covered, the roles and responsibilities of employees, and the enforcement mechanisms.

Tailor Policies to Organizational Needs:

Customize security policies and procedures to align with the organization's unique business requirements, industry regulations, and compliance standards.

Ensure that policies are practical, easy to understand, and applicable to different departments and job roles within the organization.

Establish Access Control Policies:

Develop access control policies and procedures to manage user access to systems, applications, and data based on the principle of least privilege.

Implement strong authentication mechanisms, such as multi-factor authentication (MFA), to verify the identity of users and prevent unauthorized access.

Implement Data Protection Policies:

Implement data protection policies and procedures to safeguard sensitive information from unauthorized disclosure, alteration, or destruction.

Encrypt sensitive data both in transit and at rest, and establish clear guidelines for data classification, handling, and retention.

Enforce Network Security Policies:

Enforce network security policies and procedures to protect the organization's network infrastructure from cyber threats and unauthorized access.

Implement firewalls, intrusion detection/prevention systems (IDS/IPS), and other security controls to monitor and control network traffic.

Develop Incident Response Plans:

Develop incident response plans and procedures to enable a timely and effective response to security incidents and data breaches.
Define roles and responsibilities for incident response team members, establish communication protocols, and conduct regular training and drills.

Provide Security Awareness Training:

Provide ongoing security awareness training and education to employees to ensure they understand their roles and responsibilities in maintaining cyber security.

Cover topics such as phishing awareness, password security, social engineering, and safe browsing habits.

Monitor Compliance and Enforcement:

Monitor compliance with security policies and procedures through regular audits, assessments, and monitoring activities.

Implement mechanisms for enforcing security policies, such as access controls, logging and monitoring, and disciplinary actions for policy violations.

Continuously Review and Update Policies:

Continuously review and update security policies and procedures to reflect changes in technology, regulations, and emerging threats.

Solicit feedback from stakeholders, monitor industry best practices, and incorporate lessons learned from security incidents into policy revisions.

Sudheer Kumar

Creating Comprehensive Security Policies

Creating comprehensive security policies is a critical step in establishing a robust cyber security posture within an organization. These policies provide a framework for defining expectations, procedures, and guidelines to protect sensitive information, mitigate risks, and ensure compliance with relevant regulations. As a cyber security manager, your role is to develop policies that are tailored to the organization's specific needs and effectively address its cyber security challenges. Here's an overview of the approach you can take:

Understand Organizational Needs and Objectives:

Start by gaining a thorough understanding of the organization's business objectives, operations, and risk profile. Identify the organization's assets, including systems, networks, data, and intellectual property, that require protection.

Conduct a Risk Assessment:

Conduct a comprehensive risk assessment to identify potential threats, vulnerabilities, and risks to the organization's assets. Evaluate the likelihood and potential impact of these risks to prioritize policy development efforts.

Define Policy Scope and Structure:

Define the scope and structure of the security policies, including the areas they will cover and the specific guidelines and procedures they will contain.

Consider organizing policies into categories such as access control, data protection, network security, incident response, and compliance.

Research Regulatory Requirements and Industry Best Practices:

Research applicable regulatory requirements, industry standards, and best practices related to cyber security.

Ensure that policies address relevant legal and regulatory requirements, such as GDPR, HIPAA, PCI DSS, or industry-specific regulations.

Collaborate with Stakeholders:

Collaborate with key stakeholders across the organization, including senior leadership, IT teams, legal, HR, and compliance, to gather input and ensure alignment.

Involve subject matter experts in policy development to ensure accuracy, relevance, and practicality.

Draft Policies with Clear and Concise Language:

Draft policies using clear, concise language that is easy to understand by all employees, regardless of their technical background.

Avoid jargon and technical terminology that may confuse or alienate non-technical users.

Address Key Security Areas:

Develop policies that address key security areas such as:

> Access Control: Define rules for granting and revoking access to systems, applications, and data.
> Data Protection: Establish guidelines for data classification, encryption, storage, and handling.
> Network Security: Define protocols and procedures for securing the organization's network infrastructure.
> Incident Response: Establish procedures for detecting, reporting, and responding to security incidents and breaches.
> Acceptable Use: Outline acceptable use of company resources, including internet, email, and software.
> Bring Your Own Device (BYOD): Define guidelines for securely using personal devices for work purposes.

Incorporate User Training and Awareness:

Include provisions for user training and awareness within policies to ensure employees understand their roles and responsibilities.

Provide examples, tips, and best practices to help employees comply with policy requirements.

Obtain Approval and Endorsement:

Obtain approval and endorsement of policies from senior leadership and relevant stakeholders before finalizing and implementing them.

Ensure policies are communicated effectively to all employees through training sessions, memos, and other communication channels.

Regularly Review and Update Policies:

Establish a process for regularly reviewing and updating security policies to reflect changes in technology, regulations, and business requirements.

Schedule periodic reviews and audits to ensure policies remain relevant, effective, and compliant.

By following this approach, cyber security managers can create comprehensive security policies that effectively mitigate risks, protect sensitive information, and promote a culture of security awareness and compliance within the organization.

Establishing Incident Response Plans

Establishing incident response plans is crucial for organizations to effectively detect, respond to, and recover from security incidents and data breaches. As a cyber security manager, it's your responsibility to develop comprehensive incident response plans that outline the procedures, roles, and responsibilities for responding to cyber security incidents. Here's an overview of the approach you can take:

Understand Organizational Context:

Start by understanding the organization's business objectives, critical assets, regulatory requirements, and risk tolerance. Tailor the incident response plans to align with the organization's specific needs and operational environment.

Sudheer Kumar

Define Incident Response Team:

Identify and assemble a cross-functional incident response team comprising representatives from IT, security, legal, HR, communications, and other relevant departments.

Define roles and responsibilities for each team member, including incident coordinators, technical analysts, communications liaisons, and legal advisors.

Conduct Risk Assessment:

Conduct a comprehensive risk assessment to identify potential threats, vulnerabilities, and risks to the organization's assets and operations.

Prioritize risks based on their likelihood and potential impact on the organization's business objectives and critical assets.

Develop Incident Response Plan Framework:

Develop a framework for the incident response plans, outlining the overall structure, objectives, and scope of the plans. Define the types of incidents covered by the plans, such as data breaches, malware infections, insider threats, or denial-of-service attacks.

Establish Incident Classification and Escalation Procedures:

Establish procedures for classifying and prioritizing security incidents based on their severity, impact, and urgency. Define escalation procedures for escalating incidents to higher levels of management or external authorities as needed.

Create Incident Response Procedures:

Develop detailed incident response procedures for each type of security incident, including detection, analysis, containment, eradication, and recovery steps. Define specific actions and tasks to be performed by the incident response team members at each stage of the incident response process.

Implement Communication and Notification Protocols:

Establish communication and notification protocols for informing key stakeholders, including senior leadership, employees, customers, partners, and regulatory authorities, about security incidents. Define communication channels, contact lists, and escalation procedures for notifying stakeholders in a timely and transparent manner.

Conduct Training and Exercises:

Provide regular training and awareness sessions to ensure that incident response team members understand their roles and responsibilities.

Conduct tabletop exercises and simulation drills to test the effectiveness of the incident response plans, identify areas for improvement, and build team coordination and collaboration.

Integrate with External Resources:

Establish relationships with external resources, such as incident response vendors, law enforcement agencies, and industry partners, to augment internal incident response capabilities.

Define procedures for engaging external resources during large-scale or complex security incidents that require additional expertise or resources.

Continuously Review and Update Plans:

Regularly review and update the incident response plans to reflect changes in technology, regulations, and emerging threats.

Conduct post-incident reviews and lessons learned sessions to identify areas for improvement and incorporate feedback into future revisions of the plans.

By following this approach, cyber security managers can establish incident response plans that enable organizations to effectively detect, respond to, and recover from security incidents, minimizing the impact on business operations and reputation.

Sudheer Kumar

Conducting Regular Security Audits and Assessments

Regular security audits and assessments are essential for identifying vulnerabilities, assessing risks, and ensuring the effectiveness of cyber security measures within an organization. As a cyber security manager, it's your responsibility to plan, coordinate, and oversee these audits and assessments to maintain the organization's security posture. Here's an overview of the approach you can take:

Establish Audit Objectives and Scope:

Define the objectives and scope of the security audit or assessment, considering factors such as regulatory requirements, industry standards, and organizational priorities.

Determine the systems, networks, applications, and processes to be included in the audit scope, ensuring comprehensive coverage of the organization's assets.

Identify Appropriate Audit Methodologies:

Select appropriate audit methodologies and frameworks, such as ISO 27001, NIST Cybersecurity Framework, or CIS Controls, based on the organization's needs and industry best practices.

Tailor audit methodologies to align with the organization's specific requirements and risk profile.

Develop Audit Plans and Checklists:

Develop detailed audit plans and checklists outlining the procedures, tasks, and activities to be performed during the audit or assessment.

Include specific criteria, benchmarks, and metrics for evaluating the effectiveness of security controls and measures.

Conduct Vulnerability Assessments:

Perform regular vulnerability assessments using automated scanning tools, penetration testing, and manual testing techniques.

Identify and prioritize vulnerabilities based on severity, likelihood of exploitation, and potential impact on the organization's assets and operations.

Review Security Policies and Procedures:

Review existing security policies, procedures, and controls to ensure compliance with regulatory requirements, industry standards, and best practices.

Identify gaps, inconsistencies, or deficiencies in security policies and procedures and develop recommendations for improvement.

Assess Security Controls and Measures:

Assess the effectiveness of security controls and measures, such as access controls, encryption, network segmentation, and intrusion detection systems.

Evaluate the implementation and configuration of security technologies and tools to ensure they are properly configured and functioning as intended.

Review Incident Response Preparedness:

Review incident response plans, procedures, and capabilities to assess the organization's readiness to detect, respond to, and recover from security incidents.

Conduct tabletop exercises or simulation drills to test the effectiveness of incident response plans and train incident response team members.

Evaluate Employee Awareness and Training:

Evaluate employee awareness and training programs to assess the level of understanding and adherence to security policies, procedures, and best practices.

Identify areas for improvement and develop targeted training and awareness initiatives to address knowledge gaps and reinforce security awareness.

Document Findings and Recommendations:

Document audit findings, observations, and recommendations in a comprehensive audit report, detailing identified vulnerabilities, weaknesses, and areas for improvement.

Prioritize findings based on risk severity and potential impact on the organization's security posture and operations.

Implement Corrective Actions and Follow-Up:

Develop and implement corrective actions and remediation plans to address identified vulnerabilities, weaknesses, and deficiencies.

Follow up on the implementation of corrective actions and verify their effectiveness through follow-up audits, assessments, or monitoring activities.

By following this approach, cyber security managers can ensure that regular security audits and assessments are conducted effectively, providing valuable insights into the organization's security posture and enabling proactive risk management and improvement of cyber security controls and measures.

Chapter 5

Securing Networks and Infrastructure

Securing networks and infrastructure is a critical aspect of cyber security management, as it involves protecting the organization's IT assets from unauthorized access, data breaches, and cyber threats. As a cyber security manager, your role is to develop and implement effective strategies, controls, and measures to safeguard the organization's networks and infrastructure. Here's an approach you can take:

Understand the Network and Infrastructure Landscape:

Start by gaining a comprehensive understanding of the organization's network architecture, infrastructure components, and technology stack.

Identify critical assets, systems, and data flows that need to be protected from cyber threats.

Conduct Risk Assessment and Vulnerability Scanning:

Conduct a thorough risk assessment and vulnerability scanning to identify potential risks, vulnerabilities, and weaknesses in the network and infrastructure.

Prioritize risks based on severity, likelihood of exploitation, and potential impact on the organization's operations.

Sudheer Kumar

Implement Access Control Mechanisms:

Implement strong access control mechanisms to restrict unauthorized access to network resources, systems, and data.

Use techniques such as role-based access control (RBAC), least privilege principle, and multi-factor authentication (MFA) to enforce access controls effectively.

Harden Network Devices and Infrastructure:

Harden network devices, such as routers, switches, and firewalls, by disabling unnecessary services, applying security patches and updates, and configuring secure password policies.

Implement security best practices, such as disabling unused ports, enabling logging and monitoring, and implementing encryption protocols.

Segment Networks and Implement Firewalls:

Segment networks into separate security zones to limit the scope of potential attacks and contain security incidents.

Deploy firewalls and network segmentation controls to monitor and control traffic between different network segments and enforce security policies.

Encrypt Network Traffic and Data:

Encrypt network traffic and data both in transit and at rest to protect sensitive information from unauthorized access and interception.

Use encryption protocols such as SSL/TLS for securing communication channels and implement data encryption mechanisms for protecting stored data.

Deploy Intrusion Detection and Prevention Systems (IDPS):

Deploy intrusion detection and prevention systems (IDPS) to monitor network traffic for signs of suspicious activity, intrusion attempts, and malware infections.

Configure IDPS rules and policies to detect and block known and emerging threats in real-time.

Conduct Regular Security Audits and Monitoring:

Conduct regular security audits, assessments, and penetration tests to evaluate the effectiveness of network security controls and measures.

Monitor network traffic, logs, and events using security information and event management (SIEM) systems to detect and respond to security incidents.

Establish Incident Response and Recovery Plans:

Develop incident response and recovery plans to enable a timely and effective response to security incidents and data breaches.

Define roles, responsibilities, and escalation procedures for responding to security incidents, and conduct regular drills and exercises to test the effectiveness of the plans.

Stay Updated on Emerging Threats and Technologies:

Stay informed about emerging cyber threats, vulnerabilities, and attack techniques through threat intelligence sources, industry publications, and security forums.

Continuously evaluate and implement new security technologies, tools, and best practices to enhance the organization's network security posture.

Sudheer Kumar

Implementing Firewalls, Intrusion Detection Systems, and Intrusion Prevention Systems:

Implementing firewalls, intrusion detection systems (IDS), and intrusion prevention systems (IPS) is crucial for safeguarding networks and infrastructure from unauthorized access, malicious activities, and cyber threats. As a cyber security manager, your role is to develop and implement a comprehensive strategy for deploying and managing these security solutions effectively. Here's an approach and overview for each component:

Firewalls:

Firewalls serve as the first line of defense in network security, controlling traffic between networks based on predefined security rules. They can be deployed at network perimeters, between network segments, or within hosts.

Define Firewall Objectives: Clearly define the objectives and scope of firewall deployment, including the types of traffic to be controlled and the security policies to be enforced.

Select Firewall Solutions: Choose appropriate firewall solutions based on the organization's requirements, such as traditional stateful firewalls, next-generation firewalls (NGFW), or cloud-based firewalls.

Design Firewall Rules: Design firewall rules and access control lists (ACLs) based on the principle of least privilege, allowing only necessary traffic and blocking or logging unauthorized access attempts.

Implement Redundancy and High Availability: Implement redundant firewall configurations and high availability mechanisms to ensure continuous protection and minimize single points of failure.

Monitor and Maintain Firewalls: Regularly monitor firewall logs and alerts to detect and respond to security incidents, and perform routine maintenance tasks such as software updates and configuration reviews.

Intrusion Detection Systems (IDS): Intrusion detection systems (IDS) monitor network traffic for signs of suspicious activity or potential security threats. They analyze network packets and log data to detect anomalies, known attack patterns, and unauthorized access attempts.

Assess Network Traffic: Assess network traffic patterns, protocols, and data flows to determine the placement and deployment of IDS sensors.

Select IDS Solutions: Choose IDS solutions based on the organization's requirements, such as network-based IDS (NIDS), host-based IDS (HIDS), or cloud-based IDS.

Tune and Configure IDS Rules: Tune IDS rules and signatures to reduce false positives and focus on detecting relevant security events and indicators of compromise.

Establish Incident Response Procedures: Define incident response procedures for handling IDS alerts and escalations, including investigation, analysis, and mitigation steps.

Integrate with SIEM and Threat Intelligence: Integrate IDS with security information and event management (SIEM) systems and threat intelligence feeds to enhance threat detection capabilities and correlation of security events.

Intrusion Prevention Systems (IPS):
Intrusion prevention systems (IPS) build upon the capabilities of IDS by actively blocking or mitigating detected threats in real-time. They can automatically respond to security incidents by blocking malicious traffic or applying preventive measures.

Evaluate Security Needs: Assess the organization's security needs and risk tolerance to determine the level of intrusion prevention capabilities required.

Select IPS Solutions: Choose IPS solutions that integrate with existing security infrastructure and provide granular control over security policies and actions.

Fine-tune IPS Policies: Fine-tune IPS policies and rules to balance security effectiveness with operational requirements and minimize disruption to legitimate traffic.

Implement Inline Protection: Deploy IPS in inline mode to actively block or drop malicious traffic in real-time, complementing the detection capabilities of IDS.

Monitor and Review Effectiveness: Continuously monitor and review IPS alerts and actions to evaluate effectiveness, identify false positives, and adjust policies as needed to optimize security posture.

By following this approach, cyber security managers can effectively implement firewalls, intrusion detection systems, and intrusion prevention systems to enhance network security, detect and respond to security incidents, and protect against a wide range of cyber threats. It's essential to consider the organization's specific requirements, risk profile, and operational needs when designing and deploying these security solutions. Regular monitoring, maintenance, and updates are also critical to ensuring the ongoing effectiveness of these security controls.

Protecting Data with Encryption and Access Controls

Protecting data with encryption and access controls is essential for maintaining the confidentiality, integrity, and availability of sensitive information within an organization. As a cyber security manager, your role is to develop and implement strategies, policies, and technologies to safeguard data assets effectively. Here's an approach and overview for each component:

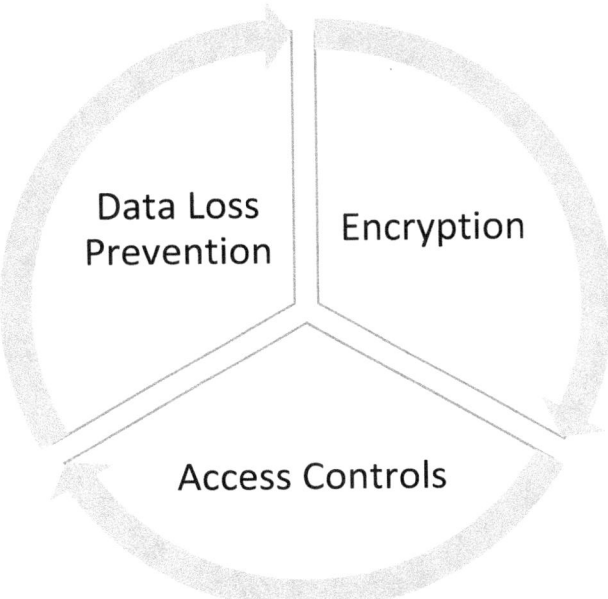

Encryption:

Encryption is the process of converting plaintext data into ciphertext to prevent unauthorized access or interception. It ensures that even if data is compromised, it remains unintelligible without the appropriate decryption key.

Identify Sensitive Data: Identify and classify sensitive data assets within the organization, including customer information, intellectual property, financial data, and personally identifiable information (PII).

Define Encryption Requirements: Define encryption requirements based on the sensitivity and criticality of data, regulatory requirements, and industry best practices.

Select Encryption Algorithms and Key Management: Choose encryption algorithms and key management practices that provide strong protection against unauthorized access and comply with relevant standards and regulations.

Implement Encryption Solutions: Implement encryption solutions for data at rest, data in transit, and data in use, using technologies such as full-disk encryption, database encryption, SSL/TLS encryption for network traffic, and application-level encryption.

Enforce Encryption Policies: Enforce encryption policies through security controls, such as data loss prevention (DLP) solutions, encryption gateways, and policy-based encryption mechanisms.

Access Controls:
Access controls are security measures that regulate and restrict access to data, systems, and resources based on user identities, roles, and permissions. They ensure that only authorized users can access and manipulate sensitive information.

Identify Access Requirements: Identify the access requirements for different data assets, systems, and applications based on business needs, regulatory requirements, and security considerations.

Define Access Control Policies: Define access control policies and principles, including the principle of least privilege, separation of duties, and role-based access control (RBAC).

Implement Authentication Mechanisms: Implement strong authentication mechanisms, such as passwords, biometrics, smart cards, and multi-factor authentication (MFA), to verify the identity of users before granting access.

Enforce Authorization Controls: Enforce authorization controls to ensure that users only have access to the data and resources necessary to perform their job functions, based on their roles and responsibilities.

Monitor and Audit Access Activities: Monitor user access activities, permissions changes, and access attempts using auditing and logging mechanisms to detect and respond to unauthorized access attempts or suspicious behavior.

Data Loss Prevention (DLP):
Data loss prevention (DLP) solutions help prevent the unauthorized disclosure of sensitive information by monitoring, detecting, and blocking the transmission of sensitive data outside the organization's network boundaries.

Identify Sensitive Data Flows: Identify and map the flow of sensitive data across the organization, including email, file transfers, web uploads, and cloud storage.

Define DLP Policies: Define DLP policies and rules to classify sensitive data, detect policy violations, and enforce data protection measures, such as encryption, blocking, or quarantine.

Deploy DLP Technologies: Deploy DLP technologies, such as email gateways, endpoint agents, network appliances, and cloud-based solutions, to monitor and control data flows and enforce DLP policies.

Educate Users and Raise Awareness: Provide training and awareness programs to educate employees about data security best practices, the importance of data protection, and their roles and responsibilities in safeguarding sensitive information.

Regularly Monitor and Fine-tune DLP Controls: Regularly monitor DLP alerts, incidents, and policy violations, and fine-tune DLP controls and policies based on feedback, analysis, and lessons learned.

By following this approach, cyber security managers can effectively protect data with encryption and access controls, mitigating the risk of data breaches, unauthorized access, and disclosure of sensitive information. It's essential to adopt a multi-layered approach to data protection, combining encryption, access controls, and DLP technologies to create robust and resilient defenses against evolving cyber threats. Regular monitoring, auditing, and review of security controls are also critical to maintaining the effectiveness of data protection measures over time.

Sudheer Kumar

Securing Cloud Infrastructure and Services

Securing cloud infrastructure and services is paramount in today's digital landscape, where organizations increasingly rely on cloud computing for their operations. As a cyber security manager, your role is to develop and implement strategies, policies, and controls to protect the organization's data, applications, and resources in the cloud. Here's an approach and overview for securing cloud infrastructure and services:

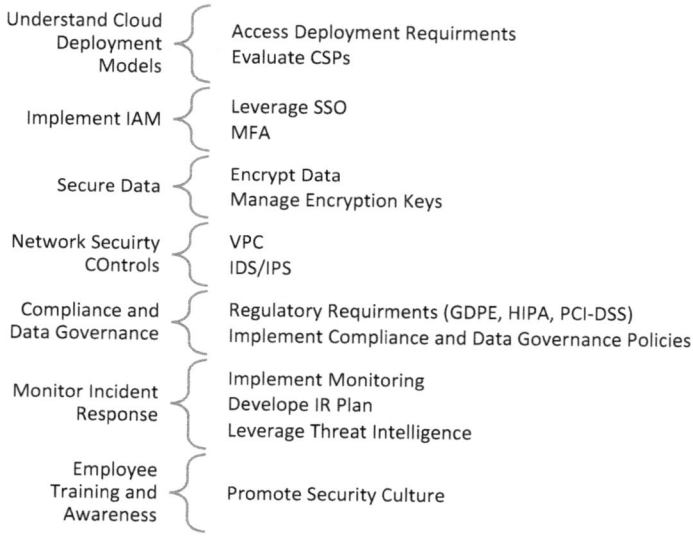

Understand Cloud Deployment Models	Access Deployment Requirments; Evaluate CSPs
Implement IAM	Leverage SSO; MFA
Secure Data	Encrypt Data; Manage Encryption Keys
Network Secuirty COntrols	VPC; IDS/IPS
Compliance and Data Governance	Regulatory Requirments (GDPE, HIPA, PCI-DSS); Implement Compliance and Data Governance Policies
Monitor Incident Response	Implement Monitoring; Develope IR Plan; Leverage Threat Intelligence
Employee Training and Awareness	Promote Security Culture

Understand Cloud Deployment Models: Cloud computing offers various deployment models, including public, private, hybrid, and multi-cloud environments. Each deployment model has unique security considerations and challenges.

Assess Deployment Requirements: Understand the organization's cloud deployment requirements, including scalability, flexibility, and data residency requirements.

Evaluate Cloud Service Providers (CSPs): Evaluate different cloud service providers (CSPs) based on their offerings, security capabilities, compliance certifications, and data protection measures.

Select Appropriate Deployment Model: Select the most suitable deployment model based on the organization's needs, risk tolerance, and regulatory requirements.

Implement Identity and Access Management (IAM):

IAM controls ensure that only authorized users and entities have access to cloud resources and data. It includes authentication, authorization, and privilege management.

Centralize Identity Management: Implement centralized identity management solutions to manage user identities, roles, and access permissions across cloud environments.

Leverage Single Sign-On (SSO): Deploy SSO solutions to enable users to authenticate once and access multiple cloud services and applications seamlessly.

Implement Multi-Factor Authentication (MFA): Enforce MFA for accessing critical cloud resources and applications to add an extra layer of security.

Secure Data in Transit and at Rest:
Data encryption ensures that sensitive data remains protected both during transmission over the network and while stored in the cloud.

Encrypt Data: Implement encryption mechanisms, such as SSL/TLS for data in transit and encryption-at-rest for data stored in cloud storage services.

Manage Encryption Keys: Securely manage encryption keys using robust key management practices to prevent unauthorized access to encrypted data.

Implement Network Security Controls:
Network security controls protect cloud infrastructure and services from unauthorized access, network-based attacks, and data breaches.

Deploy Virtual Private Cloud (VPC): Implement VPCs to create isolated network environments within the cloud, allowing organizations to define and enforce network access controls.

Use Firewalls and Intrusion Detection/Prevention Systems (IDS/IPS): Deploy firewalls and IDS/IPS solutions to monitor and control network traffic entering and leaving cloud environments, detecting and mitigating threats in real-time.

Ensure Compliance and Data Governance:
Compliance frameworks and data governance practices help ensure that cloud deployments adhere to regulatory requirements and industry standards.

Understand Regulatory Requirements: Identify applicable regulations, such as GDPR, HIPAA, PCI DSS, and industry standards relevant to the organization's industry and geography.

Implement Compliance Controls: Implement controls and measures to ensure compliance with regulatory requirements, such as data residency, data protection, and privacy regulations.

Establish Data Governance Policies: Develop data governance policies and procedures to govern the collection, storage, access, and use of data in the cloud, ensuring data integrity, confidentiality, and availability.

Monitor and Incident Response:
Continuous monitoring and incident response capabilities are crucial for detecting and responding to security incidents and breaches in the cloud.

Implement Cloud Security Monitoring: Deploy cloud-native monitoring and logging solutions to monitor cloud environments for suspicious activities, unauthorized access attempts, and security incidents.

Develop Incident Response Plan: Develop and regularly test incident response plans specific to cloud environments, defining roles, responsibilities, and procedures for responding to security incidents.

Leverage Threat Intelligence: Incorporate threat intelligence feeds and security analytics to identify emerging threats and vulnerabilities in cloud environment.

Employee Training and Awareness: Employee training and awareness programs help educate users about cloud security best practices and their role in maintaining a secure cloud environment.

Provide Cloud Security Training: Offer regular training sessions and awareness programs to educate employees about cloud security risks, policies, and procedures.

Promote Security Culture: Foster a security-aware culture within the organization, encouraging employees to follow security best practices and report suspicious activities promptly.

By following this approach, cyber security managers can effectively secure cloud infrastructure and services, mitigate risks, and protect sensitive data and resources from cyber threats and breaches in the cloud. It's essential to adopt a proactive and multi-layered approach to cloud security, combining technical controls, compliance measures, and user awareness initiatives to ensure the resilience and integrity of cloud deployments. Regular audits, assessments, and reviews are also critical to maintaining the effectiveness of cloud security controls over time.

Chapter 6

Managing Identity and Access

Managing identity and access effectively is essential for maintaining the security of an organization's digital assets and resources. As a cyber security manager, your role is to develop and implement strategies, policies, and controls to ensure that only authorized individuals have access to sensitive information and systems. Here's an approach and overview for managing identity and access:

Understand Identity and Access Management (IAM) Fundamentals

IAM involves managing digital identities, user authentication, and access controls to protect organizational resources from unauthorized access.

Define IAM Objectives: Clarify the organization's IAM objectives, considering factors such as security requirements, regulatory compliance, and operational needs.

Assess Current State: Evaluate the existing IAM processes, systems, and controls to identify strengths, weaknesses, and areas for improvement.

Establish IAM Framework: Develop an IAM framework that outlines the principles, policies, and procedures for managing identities and access across the organization.

Implement Centralized Identity Management:

Centralized identity management involves maintaining a single source of truth for user identities, roles, and access permissions.

Deploy Identity Directory Services:

Implement directory services, such as Active Directory or LDAP, to centralize user identity information and manage authentication and authorization.

Establish User Lifecycle Management:

Define processes for onboarding, provisioning, deprovisioning, and managing user accounts throughout their lifecycle, ensuring timely access management.

Enforce Strong Authentication Mechanisms:

Strong authentication mechanisms help verify the identity of users before granting access to sensitive resources.

Implement Multi-Factor Authentication (MFA):

Enforce MFA for accessing critical systems, applications, and data, requiring users to provide multiple forms of verification, such as passwords, biometrics, smart cards, or one-time passcodes.

Leverage Single Sign-On (SSO):

Deploy SSO solutions to streamline access management and improve user experience while maintaining strong authentication controls across multiple systems and applications.

Adopt Role-Based Access Control (RBAC):

RBAC assigns access permissions to users based on their roles and responsibilities within the organization, streamlining access management and reducing the risk of unauthorized access.

Define Role Hierarchies:

Define role hierarchies and permissions matrices that map user roles to specific access privileges and resources.

Assign Least Privilege:

Apply the principle of least privilege, granting users only the permissions necessary to perform their job functions, to minimize the risk of excessive access rights.

Implement Access Reviews and Auditing:

Regular access reviews and auditing help ensure that access permissions align with organizational policies and security requirements.

Conduct Periodic Access Reviews:

Conduct regular access reviews to validate user access rights, identify excessive permissions, and revoke unnecessary privileges.

Monitor Access Activities:

Implement auditing and logging mechanisms to monitor user access activities, track changes to access permissions, and detect suspicious behavior or policy violations.

Secure Privileged Access:

Privileged access management (PAM) controls and monitors access to critical systems and privileged accounts to prevent misuse or abuse.

Segment Privileged Accounts:

Segregate privileged accounts from standard user accounts and enforce strict access controls, such as just-in-time (JIT) access and session recording, for privileged users.

Implement PAM Solutions:

Deploy PAM solutions to manage, monitor, and secure privileged access to sensitive systems, applications, and data.

Provide User Training and Awareness:

User training and awareness programs help educate employees about the importance of IAM practices and their role in maintaining a secure access environment.

Offer Security Awareness Training:

Provide regular training sessions and awareness programs to educate users about IAM best practices, password hygiene, phishing awareness, and social engineering prevention.

Promote Security Culture:

Foster a culture of security awareness and accountability within the organization, encouraging employees to report suspicious activities and adhere to access management policies.

By following this approach, cyber security managers can effectively manage identity and access across the organization, mitigate the risk of unauthorized access, and protect sensitive information and resources from cyber threats and breaches. It's essential to adopt a proactive and risk-based approach to IAM, continuously monitoring and adapting access controls to align with changing business needs and evolving security threats. Regular audits, assessments, and reviews are also critical to ensuring the effectiveness of IAM controls over time.

Implementing Multi-Factor Authentication

Multi-factor authentication (MFA) is a critical security measure that adds an extra layer of protection to user accounts and systems by requiring multiple forms of verification before granting access. As a cyber security manager, implementing MFA is essential for enhancing security posture and mitigating the risk of unauthorized access and data breaches. Here's an approach and overview for implementing MFA effectively:

Assess Organizational Needs and Requirements:

Before implementing MFA, it's essential to understand the organization's specific needs, requirements, and risk profile. This includes considering factors such as the types of systems and applications used, regulatory compliance requirements, and user workflows.

Conduct Risk Assessment:

Assess the organization's risk exposure to unauthorized access and credential theft, considering the sensitivity of data and systems.

Identify User Workflows:

Identify user workflows and access patterns to determine the most appropriate MFA methods and deployment strategies.

Review Regulatory Requirements:

Review regulatory requirements and industry standards relevant to the organization's industry and geography to ensure compliance with MFA mandates.

Select MFA Methods and Technologies:

There are various MFA methods and technologies available, including one-time passwords (OTP), biometrics, smart cards, and push notifications. Choosing the right MFA methods depends on factors such as usability, security, and compatibility with existing systems.

Evaluate MFA Solutions:

Evaluate different MFA solutions and technologies based on their features, security capabilities, scalability, and ease of integration.

Consider User Experience:

Consider the user experience when selecting MFA methods, ensuring that authentication processes are user-friendly and not overly burdensome.

Ensure Compatibility:

Ensure that chosen MFA solutions are compatible with existing systems, applications, and authentication protocols to facilitate seamless integration.

Plan Deployment and Rollout:

Deploying MFA requires careful planning to minimize disruption to users and ensure smooth adoption. A phased rollout approach can help manage deployment effectively while providing adequate support and training to users.

Develop Deployment Plan:

Develop a deployment plan outlining the timeline, scope, and milestones for implementing MFA across the organization.

Define User Groups:

Define user groups and access levels to determine which users and systems will be subject to MFA requirements.

Communicate with Stakeholders:

Communicate with stakeholders, including employees, IT teams, and management, to explain the benefits of MFA and prepare them for the upcoming changes.

Provide Training and Support:

Provide training and support to users to help them understand how to enroll in MFA, use authentication methods, and troubleshoot common issues.

Configure and Integrate MFA Solutions:

Configuring and integrating MFA solutions involves setting up authentication policies, integrating MFA with existing systems and applications, and configuring user enrollment and authentication workflows.

Define Authentication Policies:

Define authentication policies specifying when and where MFA is required, such as for remote access, privileged accounts, or sensitive systems.

Integrate with Identity Management Systems:

Integrate MFA solutions with identity and access management (IAM) systems, directory services, and single sign-on (SSO) platforms to streamline user provisioning and authentication.

Configure User Enrollment:

Configure user enrollment processes to facilitate the registration and setup of MFA methods, such as sending enrollment links or tokens to users via email or SMS.

Test and Validate Configuration:

Test and validate MFA configuration settings to ensure that authentication mechanisms work as intended and provide the expected level of security.

Monitor, Evaluate, and Improve:

Monitoring MFA usage and effectiveness is essential for identifying security incidents, detecting anomalies, and continuously improving authentication controls over time.

Monitor Authentication Logs: Monitor authentication logs and events generated by MFA solutions to track user authentication attempts, identify suspicious activities, and investigate security incidents.

Analyze User Feedback:

Gather feedback from users regarding their MFA experience, usability issues, and any challenges they encounter during authentication.

Review and Adjust Policies:

Regularly review MFA policies, access controls, and authentication methods based on feedback, user behavior, and evolving security threats.

Stay Informed About Threats:

Stay informed about emerging threats, vulnerabilities, and attack techniques related to MFA, and adjust security controls accordingly to mitigate risks.

By following this approach, cyber security managers can effectively implement multi-factor authentication (MFA) to enhance security posture, protect user accounts and sensitive data, and mitigate the risk of unauthorized access and data breaches. It's essential to consider the organization's specific needs, user workflows, and regulatory requirements when implementing MFA and to continuously monitor and improve authentication controls to adapt to evolving security threats.

Managing User Access Privileges and Roles

Managing user access privileges and roles is a critical aspect of cybersecurity management, ensuring that the right individuals have appropriate access to resources while mitigating the risk of unauthorized access or misuse. Here's an approach and overview for managing user access privileges and roles effectively:

Inventory and Classification:

Begin by cataloging all resources within the organization, including applications, databases, networks, and files. Classify these resources based on sensitivity and criticality to determine the level of access control required.

Role-Based Access Control (RBAC):

Implement RBAC to assign permissions to users based on their roles and responsibilities within the organization. Define roles that reflect job functions and responsibilities, and assign appropriate access privileges to each role.

Least Privilege Principle:

Adhere to the principle of least privilege, granting users the minimum level of access required to perform their tasks. Regularly review and refine access privileges to ensure they align with current job responsibilities.

Access Reviews and Audits:

Conduct regular access reviews and audits to ensure that user access privileges remain appropriate over time. This involves reviewing access rights, identifying any discrepancies or anomalies, and revoking unnecessary privileges.

Authentication and Authorization Mechanisms:

Implement robust authentication mechanisms such as multi-factor authentication (MFA) to verify users' identities before granting access. Combine authentication with authorization mechanisms to ensure that authenticated users have appropriate access privileges.

Centralized Identity and Access Management (IAM):

Implement a centralized IAM system to manage user identities, access privileges, and authentication mechanisms centrally. This enables consistent enforcement of access controls across the organization and simplifies administration.

Segregation of Duties (SoD):

Implement SoD policies to prevent conflicts of interest and reduce the risk of fraud or errors. Ensure that no single user has the ability to carry out critical tasks without oversight or approval from other parties.

Monitoring and Incident Response:

Deploy monitoring tools to track user activity and detect any unauthorized access attempts or suspicious behavior. Establish incident response procedures to address security incidents promptly and mitigate any potential damage.

Training and Awareness:

Provide regular training and awareness programs to educate users about the importance of access control, the risks of unauthorized access, and best practices for safeguarding access credentials.

Compliance and Regulatory Requirements:

Ensure that access control measures align with relevant compliance standards and regulatory requirements applicable to your industry. Stay abreast of changes in regulations and adjust access control policies accordingly.

Continuous Improvement:

Continuously assess and refine access control policies and procedures based on evolving security threats, organizational changes, and lessons learned from security incidents.

By following these principles and practices, cyber security managers can effectively manage user access privileges and roles, reducing the risk of unauthorized access and enhancing the overall security posture of the organization.

Cyber Security Manager's Handbook

Securing Third-Party Access and Vendor Relationships

Securing third-party access and managing vendor relationships is crucial for maintaining the overall security posture of an organization. Here's an approach and overview for effectively securing third-party access and vendor relationships as a cybersecurity manager:

Vendor Risk Assessment:

Conduct thorough risk assessments of third-party vendors before engaging in business relationships. Evaluate vendors based on their security practices, compliance with relevant regulations, data protection measures, and overall cybersecurity posture.

Contractual Obligations:

Include security requirements and expectations in vendor contracts and service level agreements (SLAs). Clearly define security responsibilities, data protection measures, incident response procedures, and compliance requirements. Ensure that vendors adhere to these contractual obligations throughout the duration of the relationship.

Access Control and Authentication:

Implement robust access control mechanisms to restrict third-party access to only the resources and data necessary for their specific role or service. Utilize strong authentication methods such as multi-factor authentication (MFA) to verify the identities of third-party users before granting access.

Encryption and Data Protection:

Require vendors to encrypt sensitive data both in transit and at rest. Implement encryption protocols to protect data exchanged between the organization and third-party vendors, reducing the risk of interception or unauthorized access.

Continuous Monitoring and Auditing:

Monitor third-party access and activities regularly to detect any suspicious behaviour or unauthorized access attempts. Implement logging and auditing mechanisms to track vendor activities and ensure compliance with security policies and contractual obligations.

Vendor Security Assessments:

Conduct periodic security assessments and audits of third-party vendors to evaluate their adherence to security best practices and compliance requirements. Assess vendors' security controls, incident response capabilities, vulnerability management practices, and overall cybersecurity maturity.

Incident Response and Communication:

Establish clear incident response procedures for addressing security incidents involving third-party vendors. Define escalation paths, communication channels, and responsibilities for both the organization and the vendor in the event of a security breach or incident.

Training and Awareness:

Provide training and awareness programs to educate both internal staff and third-party vendors about security best practices, data protection measures, and compliance requirements. Foster a culture of security awareness and collaboration between the organization and its vendors.

Regulatory Compliance:

Ensure that third-party vendors comply with relevant regulatory requirements and industry standards applicable to the organization's operations. Conduct regular assessments to verify vendors' compliance with regulations such as GDPR, HIPAA, PCI DSS, or other industry-specific mandates.

Continuous Improvement:

Continuously evaluate and improve the organization's processes and procedures for managing third-party access and vendor relationships. Incorporate lessons learned from security incidents, audits, and assessments to enhance the effectiveness of security measures over time.

By following these practices and incorporating them into the organization's vendor management program, cybersecurity managers can effectively mitigate the risks associated with third-party access and maintain a secure vendor ecosystem.

Chapter 7

Monitoring and Incident Response

As a cybersecurity manager, monitoring and incident response play a crucial role in safeguarding the organization's assets and mitigating potential security threats. Here's an overview of monitoring and incident response practices:

Continuous Monitoring:

Implement robust monitoring tools and techniques to continuously monitor the organization's network, systems, and applications for signs of suspicious activity or security breaches. Utilize intrusion detection systems (IDS), intrusion prevention systems (IPS), security information and event management (SIEM) solutions, and endpoint detection and response (EDR) tools to detect and respond to security incidents in real-time.

Log Management and Analysis:

Collect and analyze logs from various sources, including network devices, servers, applications, and security appliances. Centralize log management to facilitate correlation and analysis of security events, enabling security teams to identify anomalies, trends, and potential security incidents effectively.

Threat Intelligence Integration:

Integrate threat intelligence feeds into monitoring systems to stay informed about emerging threats, vulnerabilities, and attack techniques. Leverage threat intelligence to enhance the organization's ability to detect and respond to advanced threats proactively.

Incident Detection and Triage:

Establish clear processes and procedures for incident detection and triage.

Define criteria for identifying security incidents, prioritize incidents based on severity and potential impact, and allocate resources accordingly to investigate and respond to incidents promptly.

Incident Response Planning:

Develop comprehensive incident response plans that outline roles, responsibilities, and procedures for responding to security incidents. Define escalation paths, communication channels, and coordination with internal teams and external stakeholders, such as law enforcement or regulatory authorities.

Containment and Mitigation: Act swiftly to contain and mitigate security incidents to prevent further damage or unauthorized access. Isolate affected systems, revoke compromised credentials, and implement temporary security controls to limit the impact of the incident while investigations are underway.

Forensic Analysis and Investigation: Conduct thorough forensic analysis and investigation of security incidents to determine the root cause, extent of compromise, and impact on the organization's assets. Preserve evidence, gather relevant data, and document findings to support incident response efforts and potential legal proceedings.

Communication and Reporting: Maintain transparent communication channels with internal stakeholders, executive leadership, and relevant external parties throughout the incident response process. Provide regular updates on the status of security incidents, actions taken, and remediation efforts. Prepare post-incident reports to document lessons learned, identify areas for improvement, and enhance incident response capabilities.

Post-Incident Review and Remediation:

Conduct post-incident reviews and debriefings to assess the effectiveness of incident response efforts and identify opportunities for improvement. Implement remediation measures to address gaps, strengthen security controls, and enhance incident response readiness for future incidents.

Training and Preparedness:

Provide ongoing training and awareness programs to educate employees about security best practices, incident response procedures, and their roles and responsibilities during security incidents. Conduct regular tabletop exercises and simulated incident scenarios to test the organization's incident response capabilities and readiness.

By implementing proactive monitoring practices and establishing robust incident response procedures, cybersecurity managers can effectively detect, respond to, and mitigate security incidents, thereby minimizing the impact on the organization's operations and reputation

Sudheer Kumar

Establishing Security Monitoring and Alerting Systems

Establishing robust security monitoring and alerting systems is essential for detecting and responding to potential security threats effectively. Here's an overview and approach for achieving this as a cybersecurity manager:

Assessment of Requirements:
- Conduct a thorough assessment of the organization's security requirements, risk profile, and compliance obligations.
- Identify the critical assets, systems, and data that need to be protected.
- Determine the types of security events and threats that should be monitored, such as unauthorized access attempts, malware infections, or data exfiltration.

Selecting Monitoring Tools and Technologies:
- Research and evaluate various monitoring tools and technologies that are suitable for the organization's needs and budget.
- Consider factors such as scalability, integration capabilities, ease of use, and compatibility with existing infrastructure.
- Choose a combination of tools such as SIEM (Security Information and Event Management) systems, intrusion detection systems (IDS), endpoint detection and response (EDR) solutions, and log management platforms.

Designing Monitoring Architecture:
- Design a monitoring architecture that aligns with the organization's infrastructure and security objectives.
- Determine the placement of monitoring sensors, agents, and collectors to capture relevant security data from across the network, endpoints, and cloud environments.
- Consider implementing network taps, span ports, and agent deployments for comprehensive coverage.

Defining Monitoring Policies and Rules:
- Develop monitoring policies and rules that specify what events and activities should trigger alerts.
- Customize these policies based on industry best practices, regulatory requirements, and threat intelligence.
- Fine-tune alert thresholds to minimize false positives while ensuring that critical security events are not overlooked.

Implementing Continuous Monitoring:
- Deploy monitoring tools and agents across the organization's infrastructure to enable continuous monitoring of security events and activities.
- Ensure comprehensive coverage of all critical systems, endpoints, network segments, and cloud environments.
- Monitor for anomalous behavior, indicators of compromise (IOCs), and known attack patterns.

Configuring Alerting Mechanisms:
- Configure alerting mechanisms to notify security personnel promptly when security events or anomalies are detected.
- Establish notification channels such as email, SMS, or integration with collaboration platforms.
- Implement automated escalation procedures to ensure that critical alerts are addressed promptly.

Integrating Threat Intelligence Feeds:
- Integrate threat intelligence feeds into the monitoring systems to enhance detection capabilities and provide context for security alerts.
- Incorporate feeds from reputable sources to stay informed about emerging threats, vulnerabilities, and attack trends.
- Leverage threat intelligence to prioritize response efforts and focus resources on the most significant risks.

Establishing Incident Response Procedures:
- Define incident response procedures and workflows for triaging, investigating, and responding to security alerts.
- Identify roles and responsibilities within the incident response team, including incident coordinators, analysts, and responders.
- Establish communication channels and escalation paths for incident notification and coordination.

Training and Skill Development:
- Provide training and skill development opportunities for security personnel to ensure they are proficient in using monitoring tools and interpreting security alerts.
- Conduct tabletop exercises and simulations to practice incident response procedures and improve preparedness.
- Foster a culture of collaboration, communication, and continuous learning within the security team.

Regular Evaluation and Improvement:
- Continuously monitor the performance and effectiveness of the monitoring and alerting systems.
- Conduct regular reviews and audits of alert logs, incident reports, and response metrics to identify areas for improvement.
- Update monitoring policies, adjust alerting rules, and optimize configurations based on lessons learned and emerging threats.
- By following this approach and implementing a comprehensive security monitoring and alerting system, cybersecurity managers can enhance the organization's ability to detect and respond to security threats proactively, thereby reducing the risk of data breaches, system compromises, and other security incidents.

Responding to Security Incidents and Breaches

Responding to security incidents and breaches requires a swift, coordinated, and systematic approach to minimize damage, contain the threat, and restore normal operations. Here's an overview and approach to responding to security incidents and breaches as a cybersecurity manager:

Preparation and Planning:
- Develop and maintain an incident response plan that outlines roles, responsibilities, and procedures for responding to security incidents.
- Establish an incident response team comprising individuals from various departments, including IT, security, legal, communications, and executive leadership.
- Conduct regular training and tabletop exercises to familiarize the incident response team with their roles and responsibilities and test the effectiveness of the incident response plan.

Detection and Triage:
- Utilize monitoring and detection tools to identify potential security incidents in real-time or as soon as possible.
- Triage incoming alerts to prioritize response efforts based on the severity, impact, and scope of the incident.
- Determine whether the incident represents a security breach, data breach, malware infection, unauthorized access, or other security threat.

Containment and Mitigation:
- Take immediate action to contain the incident and prevent further damage or unauthorized access.
- Isolate affected systems or networks, block suspicious activity, and revoke compromised credentials.
- Implement temporary security controls or workarounds to limit the impact of the incident while investigations are underway.

Investigation and Analysis:
- Conduct a thorough investigation to determine the root cause, attack vectors, and methods used by the threat actor. Collect and analyze forensic evidence, including logs, system snapshots, network traffic captures, and malware samples.
- Identify indicators of compromise (IOCs), malware signatures, or other artifacts associated with the incident.

Communication and Reporting:
- Notify relevant stakeholders, including executive leadership, IT teams, legal counsel, and regulatory authorities, about the incident.
- Establish communication channels and coordination mechanisms to keep stakeholders informed of the incident's status, impact, and remediation efforts.
- Prepare incident reports detailing the incident timeline, findings, impact assessment, remediation actions, and recommendations for improvement.

Remediation and Recovery:
- Develop a remediation plan to address the root causes, vulnerabilities, and weaknesses identified during the investigation.
- Prioritize remediation actions based on their criticality, feasibility, and potential impact on security.
- Implement corrective measures, such as patching systems, updating configurations, enhancing access controls, and improving security awareness training.

Post-Incident Review and Lessons Learned:
- Conduct a post-incident review to evaluate the effectiveness of the incident response efforts and identify areas for improvement.
- Document lessons learned, best practices, and recommendations for enhancing the organization's incident response capabilities.
- Incorporate feedback from the post-incident review into future incident response planning, training, and preparedness activities.

Monitoring and Continuous Improvement:
- Monitor the organization's systems, networks, and applications for any signs of recurring or new security threats.
- Conduct regular reviews and assessments to evaluate the organization's security posture and resilience to similar incidents.
- Continuously refine incident response procedures, update security policies, and adapt security measures based on emerging threats, industry best practices, and lessons learned from past incidents.

By following this approach, cybersecurity managers can effectively respond to security incidents and breaches, mitigate their impact, and strengthen the organization's overall security posture.

Conducting Post-Incident Analysis and Remediation

Conducting post-incident analysis and remediation is crucial for learning from security incidents, improving the organization's security posture, and preventing future occurrences. Here's an overview and approach for conducting post-incident analysis and remediation as a cybersecurity manager:

Immediate Response and Containment:
- Upon detecting a security incident, initiate immediate response actions to contain the incident and minimize further damage or unauthorized access.
- Isolate affected systems or networks, revoke compromised credentials, and implement temporary security controls to mitigate the impact of the incident.

Documentation and Evidence Preservation:
- Document all actions taken during the incident response process, including timestamps, decisions made, and changes implemented.
- Preserve evidence related to the incident, such as log files, system snapshots, network traffic captures, and malware samples, to support post-incident analysis and investigations.

Incident Analysis and Root Cause Identification:
- Conduct a thorough analysis of the incident to identify the root cause, attack vectors, and methods used by the threat actor.
- Review security logs, forensic data, and other relevant evidence to reconstruct the timeline of events leading up to and during the incident.
- Determine any vulnerabilities or weaknesses in the organization's security controls, processes, or procedures that contributed to the incident.

Impact Assessment:
- Assess the impact of the incident on the organization's operations, systems, data, and reputation.
- Determine the extent of data exposure, loss, or compromise resulting from the incident.
- Evaluate the financial, legal, and regulatory implications of the incident, including potential fines, penalties, or legal liabilities.

Lessons Learned and Best Practices:
- Identify key lessons learned from the incident response process, including successes, challenges, and areas for improvement.
- Document best practices and recommendations for enhancing the organization's incident response capabilities, security controls, and resilience to future incidents.
- Share lessons learned with relevant stakeholders, including executive leadership, IT teams, and incident response personnel, to promote continuous improvement and knowledge sharing.

Remediation Planning and Implementation:
- Develop a remediation plan to address the root causes, vulnerabilities, and weaknesses identified during the post-incident analysis.
- Prioritize remediation actions based on their criticality, feasibility, and potential impact on security.
- Implement corrective measures, such as patching systems, updating configurations, enhancing access controls, and improving security awareness training.

Communication and Reporting:
- Communicate findings and recommendations from the post-incident analysis to executive leadership, relevant stakeholders, and regulatory authorities as necessary.
- Provide comprehensive incident reports detailing the incident timeline, impact assessment, root cause analysis, remediation actions, and lessons learned.
- Ensure transparency and accountability in communicating the organization's response to the incident and its commitment to improving security measures.

Monitoring and Continuous Improvement:
- Monitor the effectiveness of remediation measures and security controls implemented in response to the incident.
- Conduct regular reviews and assessments to evaluate the organization's security posture and resilience to similar incidents.
- Continuously refine incident response procedures, update security policies, and adapt security measures based on emerging threats, industry best practices, and lessons learned from past incidents.

Chapter 8

Compliance and Regulatory Requirements

As a cybersecurity manager, ensuring compliance with regulatory requirements and industry standards is essential for maintaining the organization's legal and regulatory obligations, protecting sensitive data, and mitigating security risks. Here's an overview and approach for managing compliance and regulatory requirements effectively:

Understanding Regulatory Landscape:

Conduct a thorough analysis of relevant regulatory requirements, industry standards, and contractual obligations that apply to the organization's operations.
Identify key regulations such as GDPR, HIPAA, PCI DSS, SOX, FISMA, NIST, ISO 27001, and others based on the organization's industry, geography, and business activities.

Gap Analysis:
- Perform a gap analysis to assess the organization's current security posture and identify areas where it deviates from compliance requirements.

- Evaluate existing security policies, procedures, controls, and technical measures against regulatory requirements to identify gaps and deficiencies.

Developing Compliance Framework:
- Develop a comprehensive compliance framework that aligns with applicable regulatory requirements and industry best practices.
- Establish policies, procedures, and controls for data protection, access control, risk management, incident response, and other key areas to meet compliance obligations.

Implementing Security Controls:
- Implement security controls and measures to address identified gaps and deficiencies and align with compliance requirements.
- Deploy technical solutions such as encryption, access control mechanisms, intrusion detection/prevention systems, and data loss prevention (DLP) tools to safeguard sensitive information.

Data Governance and Privacy:
- Establish robust data governance practices to ensure the confidentiality, integrity, and availability of sensitive data in compliance with privacy regulations.
- Implement privacy controls, consent mechanisms, data classification, and data lifecycle management processes to protect personal and sensitive information.

Continuous Monitoring and Auditing:
- Implement continuous monitoring solutions to track compliance with regulatory requirements and detect any deviations or security incidents.
- Conduct regular audits, assessments, and reviews to evaluate the effectiveness of security controls and ensure ongoing compliance with regulatory standards.

Risk Management:
- Integrate compliance requirements into the organization's risk management framework to identify, assess, and mitigate security risks effectively.
- Prioritize remediation efforts based on the severity of non-compliance issues and the potential impact on the organization's operations and reputation.

Training and Awareness:
- Provide comprehensive training and awareness programs to educate employees about their roles and responsibilities in maintaining compliance with regulatory requirements.
- Foster a culture of compliance and security awareness throughout the organization to promote adherence to policies and procedures.

Incident Response and Reporting:
- Develop incident response procedures that align with regulatory requirements for reporting security incidents, breaches, or data breaches.
- Establish communication channels and reporting mechanisms to notify regulatory authorities, customers, and other stakeholders in accordance with regulatory timelines and requirements.

Documentation and Recordkeeping:
- Maintain accurate documentation of compliance efforts, including policies, procedures, risk assessments, audit reports, and evidence of controls implementation.
- Retain records for the required retention periods specified by regulatory authorities to demonstrate compliance during audits and inspections.

Engaging with Regulators and External Auditors:
- Foster positive relationships with regulatory authorities, industry groups, and external auditors to stay informed about changes in regulatory requirements and compliance expectations.
- Collaborate with external parties to facilitate audits, assessments, and regulatory inquiries, and address any compliance issues proactively.

Continuous Improvement:
- Continuously monitor changes in regulatory requirements, industry standards, and emerging threats to adapt compliance programs accordingly.
- Regularly review and update security policies, procedures, and controls to address evolving compliance needs and improve the organization's overall security posture.

Sudheer Kumar

Understanding Legal and Regulatory Frameworks

Understanding legal and regulatory frameworks is crucial for cybersecurity managers to ensure compliance with relevant laws, regulations, and industry standards. Here's an overview and approach to understanding legal and regulatory frameworks:

Identify Applicable Regulations and Standards:
- Conduct a comprehensive review of relevant laws, regulations, and industry standards that apply to your organization based on its geographic location, industry sector, and the nature of its operations.
- Identify key regulatory bodies and authorities responsible for overseeing cybersecurity compliance in your jurisdiction or industry.

Stay Informed About Changes and Updates:
- Regularly monitor legislative and regulatory developments to stay informed about changes, updates, and new requirements that may impact cybersecurity practices.
- Subscribe to newsletters, alerts, and publications from regulatory agencies, industry associations, and legal sources to stay up-to-date on emerging trends and developments.

Engage Legal and Compliance Teams:
- Collaborate closely with the organization's legal and compliance teams to understand the legal implications of cybersecurity regulations and requirements.
- Seek guidance from legal experts to interpret complex legal language, clarify regulatory requirements, and ensure compliance with applicable laws and regulations.

Conduct Regulatory Gap Assessments:
- Conduct regulatory gap assessments to evaluate the organization's current cybersecurity practices and controls against relevant legal and regulatory requirements.
- Identify gaps, deficiencies, or areas of non-compliance that need to be addressed to align with regulatory mandates.

Develop Compliance Roadmaps and Action Plans:
- Develop compliance roadmaps and action plans to address identified gaps and deficiencies in cybersecurity practices.

- Prioritize remediation efforts based on the severity of non-compliance, potential impact on the organization, and regulatory deadlines.

Implement Controls and Policies:
- Implement controls, policies, and procedures to address specific regulatory requirements and mitigate compliance risks.
- Ensure that cybersecurity controls align with regulatory mandates, industry best practices, and recognized frameworks such as NIST Cybersecurity Framework, ISO 27001, or CIS Controls.

Establish Compliance Monitoring and Reporting:
- Implement compliance monitoring mechanisms to track adherence to regulatory requirements and assess the effectiveness of cybersecurity controls.
- Develop reporting processes to communicate compliance status, findings, and remediation efforts to relevant stakeholders, including executive leadership, regulatory authorities, and auditors.

Conduct Regular Compliance Audits and Assessments:
- Conduct regular compliance audits and assessments to evaluate the organization's adherence to regulatory requirements and identify areas for improvement.
- Engage internal or external auditors to perform independent assessments and validate compliance efforts.

Provide Training and Awareness:
- Provide training and awareness programs to educate employees about relevant legal and regulatory requirements, cybersecurity policies, and compliance obligations.
- Ensure that employees understand their roles and responsibilities in maintaining compliance with regulatory mandates.

Maintain Documentation and Records:
- Maintain accurate and up-to-date documentation of cybersecurity policies, procedures, controls, and compliance efforts.
- Keep records of compliance assessments, audit findings, remediation activities, and communications with regulatory authorities for future reference and audit purposes.

Engage with Industry Peers and Networks:
- Participate in industry forums, conferences, and working groups to exchange insights, best practices, and lessons learned related to regulatory compliance.
- Engage with peer organizations and industry networks to benchmark cybersecurity practices and share knowledge about navigating regulatory requirements.

By following this approach, cybersecurity managers can effectively navigate legal and regulatory frameworks, ensure compliance with applicable laws and regulations, and mitigate legal risks associated with cybersecurity non-compliance.

Ensuring Compliance with Industry Standards

Ensuring compliance with industry standards such as (e.g. GDPR, HIPAA, ISO, CIS, NIST, COBIT) is essential for cybersecurity managers to protect sensitive data, mitigate risks, and maintain the trust of stakeholders. Here's a comprehensive approach to ensuring compliance with multiple industry standards:

Understand Regulatory and Standard Requirements:
- Familiarize yourself with the specific requirements outlined in each industry standard or regulation relevant to your organization.
- Identify key principles, mandates, and provisions within each standard, such as data protection requirements in GDPR, healthcare data privacy in HIPAA, or cybersecurity controls in ISO, CIS, NIST, and COBIT frameworks.

Conduct a Compliance Gap Analysis:
- Assess your organization's current cybersecurity practices, policies, and controls against the requirements outlined in each industry standard or regulation.
- Identify gaps, deficiencies, or areas of non-compliance that need to be addressed to align with regulatory mandates and standard requirements.
- Prioritize remediation efforts based on the severity of non-compliance and potential impact on the organization's operations and security posture.

Develop a Unified Compliance Roadmap:
- Develop a unified compliance roadmap that integrates requirements from multiple industry standards and regulations into a single, cohesive plan.
- Break down compliance efforts into manageable tasks, assign responsibilities to relevant stakeholders, and establish timelines for completion.
- Ensure alignment with organizational goals, budget constraints, and resource availability when developing the compliance roadmap.

Implement Cross-Cutting Security Controls and Policies:
- Implement cross-cutting security controls, policies, and procedures designed to address requirements common to multiple industry standards and regulations.

- Establish overarching security measures such as access controls, encryption protocols, incident response procedures, and risk management frameworks that comply with the requirements of each standard.

Tailor Controls to Specific Requirements:
- Tailor security controls and policies to address the specific requirements and objectives of each industry standard or regulation.
- Customize data protection measures, consent management processes, audit trails, and documentation requirements to align with the nuances of GDPR, HIPAA, ISO, CIS, NIST, COBIT, or other frameworks.

Conduct Regular Audits and Assessments:
- Conduct regular audits and assessments to evaluate the effectiveness of security controls and ensure ongoing compliance with industry standards and regulations.
- Engage internal or external auditors to perform independent assessments and validate compliance efforts across multiple standards and regulations.
- Review audit findings, identify areas for improvement, and take corrective actions to address any non-compliance issues identified during audits.

Provide Cross-Disciplinary Training and Awareness:
- Provide training and awareness programs that cover the requirements of multiple industry standards and regulations to educate employees about cybersecurity policies, compliance obligations, and best practices.
- Ensure that employees understand their roles and responsibilities in maintaining compliance with regulatory mandates and protecting sensitive data across various domains.

Maintain Documentation and Records:
- Maintain accurate and up-to-date documentation of cybersecurity policies, procedures, controls, and compliance efforts for each industry standard and regulation.
- Keep records of compliance assessments, audit findings, remediation activities, and communications with regulatory authorities to demonstrate compliance across multiple frameworks.

Monitor Changes in Regulations and Standards:
- Stay informed about changes, updates, and amendments to industry standards and regulatory requirements.
- Monitor legislative and regulatory developments to ensure that your organization remains compliant with evolving cybersecurity laws, regulations, and standards.

Engage Legal, Compliance, and Governance Teams:
- Collaborate closely with the organization's legal, compliance, and governance teams to interpret regulatory requirements, address legal implications, and ensure compliance with multiple industry standards.
- Seek guidance from legal experts, compliance officers, and governance professionals to navigate complex legal and regulatory landscapes and mitigate legal risks associated with non-compliance.

By following this comprehensive approach, cybersecurity managers can effectively ensure compliance with multiple industry standards and regulations, protect sensitive data, mitigate risks, and maintain the trust and confidence of stakeholders.

Sudheer Kumar

Navigating International Data Protection Regulations

Navigating international data protection regulations as a cybersecurity manager requires a thorough understanding of the applicable laws, compliance requirements, and best practices for protecting personal data across different jurisdictions. Here's an approach and overview for effectively managing international data protection regulations:

Identify Applicable Regulations: Identify the international data protection regulations that apply to your organization based on its geographic locations, the nature of its operations, and the jurisdictions where it conducts business.

Common international data protection regulations include the General Data Protection Regulation (GDPR) in the European Union, the California Consumer Privacy Act (CCPA) in the United States, and the Personal Data Protection Act (PDPA) in Singapore, among others.

Conduct a Compliance Gap Analysis: Conduct a comprehensive assessment of your organization's data processing activities, privacy practices, and security controls against the requirements of applicable international data protection regulations. Identify gaps, deficiencies, or areas of non-compliance that need to be addressed to align with regulatory mandates and protect personal data effectively.

Develop a Compliance Framework: Develop a compliance framework that outlines the policies, procedures, and controls necessary to comply with international data protection regulations. Incorporate principles such as data minimization, purpose limitation, data accuracy, security safeguards, and data subject rights into the compliance framework.

Establish Data Governance and Accountability: Establish clear roles and responsibilities for data governance and accountability within the organization, including data protection officers (DPOs) or privacy leads responsible for overseeing compliance efforts. Implement processes for data inventory and mapping, data classification, data impact assessments, and data lifecycle management to ensure effective governance of personal data.

Implement Privacy by Design and Default: Incorporate privacy by design and default principles into the development and deployment of products, services, and systems to embed privacy protections from the outset. Implement technical and organizational measures to minimize the collection, use, and retention of personal data, and to enhance data security and privacy.

Implement Security Controls and Safeguards: Implement robust security controls and safeguards to protect personal data against unauthorized access, disclosure, alteration, or destruction. Utilize encryption, access controls, authentication mechanisms, data loss prevention (DLP) solutions, and other security measures to mitigate data security risks effectively.

Provide Data Subject Rights and Consent Management: Develop processes for honoring data subject rights, including the rights to access, rectification, erasure, restriction of processing, data portability, and objection. Implement mechanisms for obtaining valid consent from individuals for the collection, processing, and sharing of their personal data, and provide transparent information about data processing activities.

Establish Cross-Border Data Transfer Mechanisms: Implement appropriate mechanisms for transferring personal data across borders in compliance with international data protection regulations. Utilize mechanisms such as standard contractual clauses (SCCs), binding corporate rules (BCRs), or mechanisms recognized by regulatory authorities to ensure lawful and secure data transfers.

Provide Training and Awareness: Provide training and awareness programs to educate employees about international data protection regulations, privacy policies, and compliance obligations. Ensure that employees understand their roles and responsibilities in protecting personal data and complying with regulatory requirements.

Conduct Regular Audits and Assessments: Conduct regular audits and assessments to evaluate the effectiveness of data protection measures and ensure ongoing compliance with international regulations. Engage internal or external auditors to perform independent assessments and validate compliance efforts.

Monitor Regulatory Developments: Stay informed about changes, updates, and amendments to international data protection regulations. Monitor regulatory developments, enforcement actions, and guidance issued by regulatory authorities to ensure that your organization remains compliant with evolving legal and regulatory requirements.

Engage Legal and Compliance Teams:

Collaborate closely with the organization's legal and compliance teams to interpret international data protection regulations, address legal implications, and ensure compliance with applicable laws and standards.

Seek guidance from legal experts and compliance officers to navigate complex legal and regulatory landscapes and mitigate legal risks associated with non-compliance.

By following this approach, cybersecurity managers can effectively navigate international data protection regulations, protect personal data across borders, and mitigate legal and regulatory risks associated with data processing activities

Chapter 9

Cyber Security Training and Awareness

Cybersecurity training and awareness are critical components of a comprehensive cybersecurity program, as they empower employees to recognize and mitigate security risks effectively. Here's an overview and approach for cybersecurity training and awareness as a cybersecurity manager:

Assessment of Training Needs:

Conduct an assessment to identify the specific training needs of employees based on their roles, responsibilities, and levels of access to sensitive information. Consider factors such as job function, technical proficiency, familiarity with cybersecurity concepts, and previous security incidents or breaches.

Define Training Objectives:

Define clear and measurable training objectives aligned with the organization's cybersecurity goals and priorities. Establish learning outcomes that focus on improving employees' understanding of cybersecurity risks, best practices, policies, and procedures.

Develop a Training Curriculum:
Develop a comprehensive training curriculum that covers a wide range of cybersecurity topics relevant to employees' roles and responsibilities. Include modules on phishing awareness, password security, social engineering tactics, data protection principles, secure use of technology, incident reporting procedures, and regulatory compliance requirements.

Utilize a Variety of Training Methods:
Employ a variety of training methods and formats to accommodate different learning styles and preferences. Offer online courses, interactive e-learning modules, webinars, workshops, simulations, and tabletop exercises to engage employees and reinforce key cybersecurity concepts.

Tailor Training Content: Tailor training content to address specific risks, threats, and compliance requirements relevant to the organization's industry sector, business operations, and regulatory environment.

Provide real-world examples, case studies, and practical scenarios that resonate with employees and illustrate the importance of cybersecurity in their daily work.

Promote Interactive Learning: Promote interactive learning experiences that encourage active participation, critical thinking, and problem-solving skills. Incorporate quizzes, assessments, group discussions, and hands-on exercises to reinforce learning objectives and measure knowledge retention.

Engage Senior Leadership Support: Secure buy-in and support from senior leadership to emphasize the importance of cybersecurity training and awareness throughout the organization.

Encourage executive sponsorship, participation in training sessions, and endorsement of cybersecurity initiatives to foster a culture of security awareness from the top down.

Foster a Culture of Security Awareness: Foster a culture of security awareness and responsibility among employees by emphasizing the role that everyone plays in protecting the organization's assets and data.

Encourage open communication, collaboration, and sharing of security-related information and concerns among employees.

Provide Ongoing Training and Refreshers: Offer ongoing cybersecurity training and refresher courses to reinforce key concepts, address emerging threats, and keep employees informed about the latest cybersecurity trends and best practices.

Schedule regular training sessions, lunch-and-learns, and awareness campaigns to maintain employees' vigilance and awareness of cybersecurity risks.

Measure Training Effectiveness: Measure the effectiveness of cybersecurity training programs through assessments, surveys, quizzes, and feedback mechanisms.

Track metrics such as completion rates, knowledge improvement, incident reporting trends, and security behavior changes to gauge the impact of training initiatives.

Continuous Improvement: Continuously evaluate and improve cybersecurity training programs based on feedback, lessons learned, and emerging threats.

Incorporate insights from security incidents, audit findings, and employee feedback to enhance training content, delivery methods, and effectiveness over time.

By following this approach, cybersecurity managers can develop and implement effective cybersecurity training and awareness programs that empower employees to become proactive defenders against cyber threats and contribute to a culture of security within the organization

Chapter 10

Emerging Technologies and Trends

Staying abreast of emerging technologies and trends is critical for cybersecurity managers to anticipate and mitigate potential threats to their organization's systems and data. Here's an overview and approach for managing emerging technologies and trends effectively:

Continuous Learning and Research:

Dedicate time to stay updated on emerging technologies, cybersecurity trends, and threat landscapes through industry publications, research papers, conferences, webinars, and online forums.

Follow reputable sources such as cybersecurity blogs, vendor advisories, threat intelligence feeds, and industry reports to stay informed about the latest developments.

Establish a Technology Watch Program:

Establish a formal technology watch program within the cybersecurity team to monitor emerging technologies and assess their potential impact on the organization's security posture.

Assign team members to track specific technology domains or industry sectors and report on relevant trends, vulnerabilities, and security implications.

Collaborate with IT and Innovation Teams:

Collaborate closely with IT teams, innovation departments, and business units to identify upcoming technology initiatives, pilot projects, or adoption of new technologies within the organization.
Participate in technology planning sessions, project reviews, and risk assessments to provide cybersecurity input and ensure that security considerations are integrated into new technology deployments from the outset.

Conduct Risk Assessments and Impact Analysis:

Conduct risk assessments and impact analysis for emerging technologies to identify potential security risks, vulnerabilities, and threat vectors.

Evaluate the security implications of adopting new technologies, including cloud computing, Internet of Things (IoT), artificial intelligence (AI), machine learning (ML), blockchain, and quantum computing, among others.

Implement Security by Design and Default:

Advocate for the adoption of security by design and default principles in the development and deployment of emerging technologies.

Work closely with technology teams to integrate security controls, privacy protections, and resilience measures into new technology architectures, systems, and applications.

Develop Security Guidelines and Best Practices:

Develop security guidelines, best practices, and standards for securely deploying, configuring, and managing emerging technologies.

Provide clear guidance on security requirements, configuration settings, access controls, encryption, authentication, and monitoring practices tailored to specific technology domains.

Provide Training and Awareness:

Provide training and awareness programs to educate employees, developers, and technology stakeholders about the security implications of emerging technologies. Offer specialized training on topics such as secure coding practices, threat modeling, vulnerability management, and incident response tailored to the organization's technology stack and business needs.

Engage with Industry Partners and Communities:

Engage with industry partners, cybersecurity communities, and professional associations to share insights, collaborate on threat intelligence sharing, and exchange best practices related to emerging technologies.

Participate in industry working groups, information-sharing platforms, and collaborative initiatives focused on addressing security challenges associated with new and emerging technologies.

Monitor Regulatory and Compliance Requirements:

Stay informed about regulatory and compliance requirements relevant to emerging technologies, such as data protection regulations, industry standards, and sector-specific mandates.

Ensure that new technology initiatives comply with applicable laws, regulations, and industry standards, and proactively address privacy, security, and compliance concerns.

Adapt and Evolve Security Strategies:

Continuously adapt and evolve cybersecurity strategies, policies, and controls to address evolving threats and challenges posed by emerging technologies.

Regularly review and update security measures in response to changes in technology landscapes, threat landscapes, and regulatory environments.

By following this approach, cybersecurity managers can effectively manage the security risks associated with emerging technologies, ensure that security considerations are integrated into technology initiatives from the outset, and support the organization's innovation and digital transformation efforts while maintaining a strong security posture.

Artificial Intelligence and Machine Learning in Cyber Security

Artificial Intelligence (AI) and Machine Learning (ML) have become increasingly important in cybersecurity due to their ability to analyze vast amounts of data, detect patterns, and identify anomalies indicative of potential security threats. As a cybersecurity manager, understanding the role of AI and ML in cybersecurity and implementing them effectively is crucial. Here's an overview and approach for leveraging AI and ML in cybersecurity:

Understanding AI and ML in Cybersecurity:

Gain a thorough understanding of AI and ML concepts, algorithms, and techniques relevant to cybersecurity.
Learn about the various applications of AI and ML in cybersecurity, including threat detection, anomaly detection, behavior analysis, malware detection, and predictive analytics.

Identifying Use Cases:

Identify specific cybersecurity use cases where AI and ML can provide value and enhance existing security capabilities.

Examples of use cases include identifying and mitigating advanced persistent threats (APTs), detecting insider threats, analyzing network traffic for suspicious behavior, and predicting security incidents based on historical data.

Selecting AI and ML Tools and Technologies:

Research and evaluate AI and ML tools, platforms, and technologies suitable for cybersecurity applications.

Choose tools that offer capabilities such as data preprocessing, feature extraction, model training, anomaly detection, and real-time threat analysis. Consider factors such as scalability, performance, accuracy, and ease of integration with existing security infrastructure.

Data Preparation and Feature Engineering:

Prepare and preprocess cybersecurity data to make it suitable for AI and ML analysis. Perform feature engineering to extract relevant features from raw data sources, such as log files, network traffic, and system telemetry.

Ensure data quality, completeness, and consistency to improve the accuracy and reliability of ML models.

Model Development and Training: Develop ML models tailored to specific cybersecurity use cases, such as intrusion detection, malware classification, or user behavior analysis.

Select appropriate algorithms, such as supervised learning, unsupervised learning, or reinforcement learning, based on the nature of the problem and available data.

Train ML models using labeled datasets or historical data to learn patterns and relationships indicative of security threats.

Integration with Security Infrastructure: Integrate AI and ML capabilities into existing security infrastructure, such as SIEM (Security Information and Event Management) systems, endpoint security solutions, and threat intelligence platforms.

Leverage APIs, plugins, or custom integrations to enable seamless communication and data exchange between AI/ML tools and other security tools.

Continuous Monitoring and Improvement: Continuously monitor the performance of AI and ML models in detecting and responding to security threats.

Analyze model outputs, evaluate detection accuracy, and refine models based on feedback from real-world incidents and security operations.

Implement mechanisms for adaptive learning and model retraining to keep ML models up-to-date and effective against evolving threats.

Security and Ethical Considerations: Consider security and ethical implications when deploying AI and ML in cybersecurity, such as data privacy, bias, transparency, and interpretability of ML models.

Implement security controls to protect AI and ML systems from adversarial attacks, data poisoning, and model manipulation.

Ensure compliance with regulatory requirements and ethical guidelines governing the use of AI and ML in cybersecurity.

Training and Skill Development: Provide training and skill development opportunities for cybersecurity professionals to acquire knowledge and expertise in AI and ML technologies.

Foster a culture of innovation, collaboration, and continuous learning within the cybersecurity team to leverage AI and ML effectively in security operations.

Collaboration and Knowledge Sharing: Collaborate with AI/ML experts, data scientists, and researchers to leverage their expertise in developing and deploying AI-powered cybersecurity solutions.

Participate in industry forums, conferences, and working groups to share insights, best practices, and lessons learned about AI and ML in cybersecurity.

By following this approach, cybersecurity managers can effectively harness the power of AI and ML to enhance threat detection, improve incident response, and strengthen the overall security posture of their organizations.

Sudheer Kumar

Approach for Addressing IoT Security Challenges

Addressing IoT (Internet of Things) security challenges requires a proactive and multi-layered approach to mitigate risks associated with the proliferation of connected devices. As a cybersecurity manager, here's an approach you can take to address IoT security challenges effectively:

Asset Discovery and Inventory: Implement tools and processes for continuous asset discovery and inventory management to identify all IoT devices connected to the organization's network.

Maintain an up-to-date inventory of IoT devices, including information such as device type, manufacturer, firmware version, and associated risks.

Risk Assessment and Classification: Conduct risk assessments to evaluate the security risks associated with each IoT device based on factors such as device type, connectivity, data sensitivity, and potential impact on the organization.

Classify IoT devices into risk categories (e.g., low, medium, high) based on their criticality and exposure to security threats.

Secure Deployment and Configuration: Develop and enforce security policies and standards for the deployment and configuration of IoT devices. Implement secure default configurations, change default passwords, disable unnecessary features, and apply firmware updates and patches regularly to mitigate known vulnerabilities.

Network Segmentation and Isolation: Segment IoT devices into separate network zones or VLANs (Virtual Local Area Networks) to isolate them from critical systems and sensitive data.

Implement network segmentation controls to restrict communication between IoT devices and limit the potential impact of a compromised device.

Access Control and Authentication: Implement strong access controls and authentication mechanisms to prevent unauthorized access to IoT devices and sensitive data.

Utilize methods such as strong passwords, multi-factor authentication (MFA), and certificate-based authentication to verify the identity of users and devices.

Data Protection and Encryption: Encrypt data transmitted between IoT devices and backend systems to protect it from eavesdropping and interception.

Implement encryption protocols such as SSL/TLS (Secure Sockets Layer/Transport Layer Security) and AES (Advanced Encryption Standard) to secure data in transit and at rest.

Continuous Monitoring and Threat Detection: Deploy IoT-specific monitoring tools and intrusion detection systems (IDS) to monitor network traffic, device behavior, and anomalies indicative of security threats.

Implement real-time alerting mechanisms to notify security teams of suspicious activities or potential security incidents involving IoT devices.

Incident Response and Remediation: Develop incident response procedures specifically tailored to address security incidents involving IoT devices. Establish protocols for isolating compromised devices, conducting forensic analysis, and remediating security vulnerabilities promptly.

Collaborate with device manufacturers, vendors, and industry partners to address security vulnerabilities and apply patches or mitigations effectively.

Employee Training and Awareness: Provide training and awareness programs to educate employees about IoT security risks, best practices, and security protocols. Emphasize the importance of adhering to security policies, recognizing potential threats, and reporting suspicious activities related to IoT devices.

Regulatory Compliance and Standards Adherence: Ensure compliance with relevant regulatory requirements and industry standards governing IoT security, such as the IoT Security Foundation's guidelines or industry-specific regulations.

Stay informed about emerging regulations and standards related to IoT security and adjust security practices accordingly to maintain compliance.

Vendor Risk Management: Evaluate the security posture of IoT device vendors and suppliers before procuring or deploying their products.

Consider factors such as the vendor's security practices, vulnerability management processes, and commitment to security updates and support.

Collaboration and Information Sharing: Collaborate with industry peers, cybersecurity organizations, and government agencies to share threat intelligence, best practices, and lessons learned related to IoT security.

Participate in industry forums, working groups, and information-sharing initiatives to stay abreast of emerging threats and trends in IoT security.

By adopting this comprehensive approach, cybersecurity managers can effectively address IoT security challenges and mitigate risks associated with the growing proliferation of connected devices within their organizations.

Sudheer Kumar

Navigating the Risks and Opportunities of Blockchain Technology

Navigating the risks and opportunities of blockchain technology requires a comprehensive understanding of its unique characteristics, potential benefits, and associated security challenges. As a cybersecurity manager, here's an approach and overview for effectively managing blockchain-related risks and opportunities:

Understanding Blockchain Technology:

Gain a thorough understanding of blockchain technology, including its underlying principles, architecture, and cryptographic mechanisms.

Learn about the different types of blockchains (public, private, and consortium) and their respective use cases in various industries.

Identifying Use Cases and Opportunities:

Identify potential use cases for blockchain technology within your organization or industry that can offer operational efficiencies, transparency, and trust. Evaluate the potential benefits of blockchain for use cases such as supply chain management, identity verification, smart contracts, and decentralized finance.

Assessing Risks and Security Challenges:

Conduct a risk assessment to identify potential security risks and challenges associated with blockchain technology, including smart contract vulnerabilities, consensus mechanisms, and regulatory compliance.

Assess the impact of blockchain-related risks on the organization's assets, operations, and reputation.

Implementing Security Controls and Best Practices: Implement security controls and best practices to mitigate risks associated with blockchain technology, such as:

- Secure development practices for smart contracts, including code review, testing, and auditing. Secure key management practices to protect private keys and digital assets.

- Network security measures to prevent unauthorized access and data breaches.
- Compliance with regulatory requirements, such as GDPR, AML/KYC, and data protection laws.

Leverage blockchain-specific security tools and technologies, such as blockchain analytics platforms, secure wallets, and permissioned blockchain frameworks.

Establishing Governance and Compliance Frameworks: Develop governance and compliance frameworks tailored to the organization's use of blockchain technology.

Define roles and responsibilities for managing blockchain projects, including governance bodies, stakeholders, and compliance officers.

Ensure compliance with relevant regulatory requirements and industry standards governing blockchain technology, such as ISO/IEC 27001, NIST SP 800-171, and FATF guidelines.

Monitoring and Incident Response: Implement monitoring and incident response procedures to detect and respond to security incidents related to blockchain technology. Monitor blockchain networks for suspicious activities, unauthorized transactions, and potential security breaches.

Establish incident response plans and protocols for investigating and mitigating security incidents involving blockchain technology.

Training and Awareness: Provide training and awareness programs to educate employees about blockchain technology, its potential benefits, and associated security risks. Train developers, IT staff, and security professionals on secure development practices, blockchain security concepts, and risk mitigation strategies.

Collaboration and Information Sharing: Collaborate with industry peers, blockchain consortia, and cybersecurity organizations to share threat intelligence, best practices, and lessons learned related to blockchain security.

Participate in industry forums, working groups, and conferences focused on blockchain security to stay informed about emerging threats and trends.

Continuous Evaluation and Improvement: Continuously evaluate the effectiveness of security controls and risk mitigation measures implemented for blockchain technology.

Conduct regular reviews and assessments to identify areas for improvement and address evolving security threats.

Incorporate feedback from security audits, incident investigations, and regulatory compliance assessments to enhance the organization's blockchain security posture over time.

By adopting this approach, cybersecurity managers can effectively navigate the risks and opportunities of blockchain technology, enabling their organizations to leverage its transformative potential while mitigating security risks and ensuring regulatory compliance

Chapter 11

Cyber Security Governance and Leadership

As a cybersecurity manager, establishing effective governance and leadership is essential for ensuring that cybersecurity initiatives align with organizational objectives, mitigate risks effectively, and promote a culture of security throughout the organization. Here's an approach and overview for cybersecurity governance and leadership:

Understand Organizational Objectives and Risk Appetite:

Gain a comprehensive understanding of the organization's mission, objectives, and strategic priorities. Identify key stakeholders, including executive leadership, board members, department heads, and business units, and understand their expectations, concerns, and risk appetite regarding cybersecurity.

Define Cybersecurity Governance Framework:

Establish a cybersecurity governance framework that outlines the structure, processes, and accountability mechanisms for managing cybersecurity within the organization.

Define roles and responsibilities for cybersecurity governance, including executive sponsors, steering committees, and working groups tasked with overseeing cybersecurity initiatives and decision-making.

Develop Cybersecurity Policies and Standards:

Develop and implement cybersecurity policies, standards, and guidelines that align with industry best practices, regulatory requirements, and organizational objectives.
Address key areas such as data protection, access control, incident response, business continuity, third-party risk management, and compliance.

Risk Management and Assessment:

Implement a risk management framework for identifying, assessing, prioritizing, and mitigating cybersecurity risks across the organization. Conduct regular risk assessments to identify vulnerabilities, threats, and potential impacts to critical assets and operations.

Establish risk tolerance levels and criteria for risk acceptance, transfer, mitigation, and avoidance based on the organization's risk appetite.

Establish Metrics and Performance Indicators:

Define cybersecurity metrics and key performance indicators (KPIs) to measure the effectiveness, efficiency, and impact of cybersecurity initiatives.

Monitor and report on cybersecurity performance against established metrics, providing regular updates to executive leadership and stakeholders on the organization's security posture and risk exposure.

Incident Response and Management:

Develop and maintain an incident response plan and procedures for detecting, analyzing, responding to, and recovering from cybersecurity incidents.

Establish incident response teams, roles, and responsibilities, and conduct regular drills and exercises to test and validate the incident response capabilities.

Training and Awareness:

Provide ongoing cybersecurity training and awareness programs to educate employees, contractors, and partners about cybersecurity risks, policies, and best practices.

Foster a culture of security awareness and accountability throughout the organization, encouraging individuals to report suspicious activities and adhere to security policies and procedures.

Vendor and Third-Party Risk Management:

Establish processes and controls for assessing and managing cybersecurity risks associated with vendors, suppliers, and third-party service providers.

Conduct due diligence assessments, contractual reviews, and ongoing monitoring of third-party security practices to ensure compliance with cybersecurity requirements and standards.

Compliance and Regulatory Requirements:

Ensure compliance with relevant cybersecurity laws, regulations, and industry standards applicable to the organization's operations, such as GDPR, HIPAA, PCI DSS, ISO 27001, and NIST Cybersecurity Framework.

Establish processes for conducting compliance assessments, audits, and reporting to demonstrate adherence to regulatory requirements and industry standards.

Continuous Improvement and Adaptation:

Foster a culture of continuous improvement and adaptation, regularly reviewing and updating cybersecurity governance practices, policies, and controls to address evolving threats, technologies, and business needs.

Incorporate lessons learned from cybersecurity incidents, audits, and assessments into the organization's cybersecurity governance framework to enhance resilience and effectiveness over time.

Engaging with Executive Leadership and Board of Directors

Engaging with executive leadership and the board of directors is essential for cybersecurity managers to ensure alignment between cybersecurity initiatives and organizational goals, secure necessary resources, and gain support for strategic decisions. Here's an approach and overview for effectively engaging with executive leadership and the board:

Understand Business Objectives and Risks:

Gain a deep understanding of the organization's business objectives, strategic priorities, and risk appetite. Identify key business processes, assets, and stakeholders that may be impacted by cybersecurity risks.

Align cybersecurity goals and initiatives with broader organizational objectives to demonstrate value and relevance to executive leadership and the board.

Establish Clear Communication Channels:

Establish regular communication channels and touchpoints with executive leadership and the board to provide updates on cybersecurity matters. Schedule periodic briefings, presentations, or workshops to educate leadership about cybersecurity risks, trends, and strategic priorities.

Ensure that cybersecurity messages are communicated effectively, using language and metrics that resonate with the audience and tie back to business objectives.

Demonstrate Business Value and ROI:

Translate cybersecurity initiatives into tangible business outcomes and value propositions that resonate with executive leadership and the board.

Quantify the potential impact of cybersecurity risks on the organization's financial, operational, and reputational resilience.

Present business cases and ROI analyses for cybersecurity investments, demonstrating how they contribute to risk reduction, operational efficiency, and competitive advantage.

Provide Strategic Guidance and Advice:

Serve as a trusted advisor to executive leadership and the board on cybersecurity matters, providing strategic guidance and recommendations to support informed decision-making.

Offer insights into emerging cybersecurity threats, regulatory developments, and industry trends that may impact the organization's risk profile and strategic direction.

Collaborate with executive leadership and the board to develop and refine cybersecurity strategies, policies, and governance frameworks that align with business goals and risk tolerance.

Facilitate Risk Management and Governance:

Facilitate discussions on cybersecurity risk management and governance at the executive and board levels, ensuring that cybersecurity risks are adequately understood, assessed, and managed.

Provide regular updates on the organization's cybersecurity posture, including risk assessments, compliance status, incident trends, and remediation progress.

Collaborate with executive leadership and the board to establish governance structures, policies, and metrics for overseeing cybersecurity risk management and accountability.

Promote a Culture of Cybersecurity Awareness and Accountability:

Advocate for a culture of cybersecurity awareness, responsibility, and accountability throughout the organization, starting from the top down.

Encourage executive leadership and the board to lead by example in prioritizing cybersecurity and adhering to established policies and practices.

Support initiatives to integrate cybersecurity considerations into decision-making processes, business planning, and performance evaluations across all levels of the organization.

Stay Informed and Engaged:

Stay informed about industry best practices, regulatory requirements, and emerging trends in cybersecurity governance and leadership.

Participate in professional networks, industry forums, and training programs to exchange insights, benchmark against peers, and enhance leadership skills.

Engage with executive leadership and the board proactively, seeking input, feedback, and support for cybersecurity initiatives, and demonstrating a commitment to collaboration and transparency.

By following this approach, cybersecurity managers can effectively engage with executive leadership and the board, fostering a culture of cybersecurity governance and leadership that enhances organizational resilience and supports strategic objectives.

Communicating the Value of Cyber Security Investments

Communicating the value of cybersecurity investments effectively is crucial for gaining support and securing necessary resources from executive leadership and stakeholders. Here's an approach and overview for conveying the value of cybersecurity investments as a security manager:

Understand Business Objectives and Risk Landscape:

Start by understanding the organization's business objectives, strategic priorities, and risk tolerance.

Identify key assets, processes, and stakeholders that may be impacted by cybersecurity risks.
Assess the current state of the organization's cybersecurity posture, including vulnerabilities, threats, and potential impact on business operations.

Quantify Potential Risks and Impacts:

Quantify the potential financial, operational, and reputational risks associated with cybersecurity threats and incidents. Estimate the potential costs of data breaches, downtime, regulatory fines, legal liabilities, and reputational damage that could result from inadequate cybersecurity measures.

Use data-driven analysis and risk assessment methodologies to prioritize cybersecurity investments based on their potential risk reduction and return on investment (ROI).

Align Investments with Business Objectives:

Align cybersecurity investments with the organization's business objectives and strategic priorities. Demonstrate how cybersecurity initiatives contribute to achieving business goals, protecting critical assets, and enhancing organizational resilience.

Highlight the strategic importance of cybersecurity as a key enabler of digital transformation, innovation, and competitive differentiation in today's interconnected business environment.

Sudheer Kumar

Highlight Regulatory Compliance Requirements:

Highlight regulatory compliance requirements and industry standards relevant to the organization's business operations. Emphasize the importance of cybersecurity investments in meeting compliance obligations, avoiding regulatory penalties, and maintaining trust with customers, partners, and stakeholders.

Provide examples of regulatory fines, legal settlements, and reputational damage incurred by organizations that have failed to comply with cybersecurity regulations.

Articulate Business Benefits and Value Proposition:

Articulate the business benefits and value proposition of cybersecurity investments in clear, tangible terms.

Highlight the positive impact of cybersecurity measures on business continuity, operational efficiency, customer trust, brand reputation, and competitive advantage.

Illustrate how cybersecurity investments can help the organization differentiate itself in the marketplace, attract new customers, and retain existing ones by demonstrating a commitment to security and data privacy.

Provide Cost-Benefit Analysis and ROI Metrics:

Provide a cost-benefit analysis and ROI metrics to justify cybersecurity investments and demonstrate their economic value.

Calculate the potential cost savings, risk reduction, and ROI associated with implementing specific cybersecurity measures, such as security controls, technologies, training programs, or
incident response capabilities.

Present investment options and alternatives, comparing their costs, benefits, and potential ROI to help decision-makers make informed choices about resource allocation.

Tailor Messaging to Audience and Stakeholders:

Tailor communication and messaging about cybersecurity investments to the specific interests, concerns, and priorities of different stakeholders, including executive leadership, board members, department heads, and external partners.

Use language and metrics that resonate with each audience, focusing on the aspects of cybersecurity that are most relevant and impactful to their roles and responsibilities.

Engage stakeholders in dialogue and collaboration to solicit input, address questions, and build consensus around cybersecurity priorities and investment decisions.

Demonstrate Continuous Improvement and Accountability:

Demonstrate a commitment to continuous improvement and accountability by monitoring the effectiveness of cybersecurity investments and measuring their impact over time.

Track key performance indicators (KPIs) and metrics related to cybersecurity outcomes, such as incident detection and response times, compliance status, risk mitigation efforts, and cost savings.

Provide regular updates and reports to executive leadership and stakeholders on the progress and results of cybersecurity initiatives, highlighting successes, lessons learned, and areas for improvement.

By following this approach, security managers can effectively communicate the value of cybersecurity investments to executive leadership and stakeholders, gaining support and commitment for initiatives that enhance organizational resilience and protect critical assets from cyber threats.

Sudheer Kumar

Building Trust and Credibility as a Cyber Security Leader

Building trust and credibility as a cybersecurity leader is crucial for effectively leading teams, influencing stakeholders, and driving positive change within an organization. Here's an approach and overview for achieving this:

Lead by Example: Demonstrate integrity, honesty, and ethical behavior in all interactions. Consistently adhere to cybersecurity policies and best practices, serving as a role model for others to follow.

Be Transparent and Authentic:

Foster open communication and transparency by sharing information openly and honestly.

Acknowledge mistakes and vulnerabilities, and communicate openly about cybersecurity challenges and risks.

Establish Expertise and Knowledge:

Continuously invest in learning and development to stay current with evolving cybersecurity trends, threats, and technologies.

Demonstrate expertise and thought leadership through certifications, training, publications, and speaking engagements.

Build Relationships and Collaborate:

Cultivate positive relationships with stakeholders across the organization, including IT teams, business units, executive leadership, and external partners.

Collaborate effectively with cross-functional teams, leveraging diverse perspectives and expertise to achieve common goals.

Listen Actively and Empathize:

Practice active listening and empathy to understand the needs, concerns, and perspectives of others.

Demonstrate empathy towards individuals impacted by cybersecurity decisions or initiatives, fostering trust and rapport.

Deliver Results and Value:

Focus on delivering tangible results and value through cybersecurity initiatives that align with organizational goals and priorities.

Quantify the impact of cybersecurity investments in terms of risk reduction, cost savings, efficiency gains, and business enablement.

Communicate Effectively:

Tailor communication to different audiences, using language and messaging that resonates with their interests and priorities.

Clearly articulate the value proposition of cybersecurity initiatives, emphasizing the benefits and outcomes for the organization.

Be Proactive and Responsive: Anticipate challenges and proactively address them before they become significant issues. Respond promptly to inquiries, concerns, and incidents, demonstrating a commitment to accountability and responsiveness.

Seek Feedback and Continuous Improvement:

Solicit feedback from stakeholders and team members regularly, and use it to identify areas for improvement and opportunities for growth.

Embrace a mindset of continuous improvement, adapting to feedback and evolving circumstances to enhance leadership effectiveness.

Celebrate Successes and Recognize Contributions:

Celebrate achievements and milestones, recognizing the efforts and contributions of individuals and teams. Foster a culture of appreciation and recognition, reinforcing positive behaviors and reinforcing a sense of accomplishment.

By following this approach, cybersecurity leaders can build trust and credibility within their organizations, fostering collaboration, engagement, and a shared commitment to cybersecurity excellence.

Chapter 12:

Future Outlook and Continuous Improvement

Anticipating Future Threats and Challenges

Anticipating future threats and challenges is a critical aspect of effective cybersecurity management. As a cybersecurity manager, here's an approach and overview for staying ahead of emerging threats and challenges:

Continuous Threat Intelligence Gathering:

Establish a robust threat intelligence program to monitor, collect, and analyze information about emerging cyber threats, attack vectors, and adversary tactics, techniques, and procedures (TTPs).

Leverage a variety of sources, including industry reports, security blogs, government advisories, information sharing forums, and commercial threat intelligence feeds.

Stay informed about geopolitical events, economic trends, and technological advancements that may influence the cybersecurity landscape.

Scenario Planning and Risk Assessment:

Conduct scenario-based risk assessments to identify potential future threats and vulnerabilities that could impact the organization's systems, data, and operations.

Develop realistic threat scenarios based on emerging trends, threat actor motivations, and known vulnerabilities relevant to the organization's industry, geography, and technology stack.
Assess the likelihood and potential impact of each threat scenario, considering factors such as attack vectors, exploitability, and potential business consequences.

Technology and Infrastructure Review:

Regularly assess the organization's technology infrastructure, including networks, systems, applications, and cloud services, to identify potential security gaps, misconfigurations, and vulnerabilities.

Stay abreast of emerging technologies and trends, such as cloud computing, IoT, AI/ML, and blockchain, and evaluate their security implications and risks.

Conduct security architecture reviews and threat XXXodelling exercises to identify weaknesses and design flaws in the organization's technology stack.

Collaboration and Information Sharing:

Foster collaboration and information sharing with peer organizations, industry groups, government agencies, and cybersecurity communities to exchange insights, threat intelligence, and best practices.

Participate in threat intelligence sharing platforms, such as ISACs (Information Sharing and Analysis Centers), sector-specific forums, and community-driven initiatives, to access timely and relevant threat intelligence.

Engage with law enforcement agencies, CERTs (Computer Emergency Response Teams), and other trusted partners to report and respond to cyber threats and incidents effectively.

Strategic Planning and Investment:

Develop a strategic cybersecurity roadmap that aligns with the organization's overall business objectives, risk tolerance, and budgetary constraints.

Prioritize cybersecurity investments based on the organization's risk profile, threat landscape, and critical assets, focusing on areas with the highest impact and likelihood of future threats.

Advocate for adequate resources, budget, and executive support to implement proactive security measures, such as threat detection and response capabilities, security awareness training, and security-by-design principles.

Cybersecurity Culture and Awareness:

Cultivate a cybersecurity-aware culture within the organization by promoting awareness, education, and training among employees, contractors, and third-party vendors.

Encourage a mindset of vigilance and resilience, empowering individuals to recognize and report potential security incidents, phishing attempts, and suspicious activities.

Conduct tabletop exercises and simulation drills to test the organization's incident response readiness and improve coordination and communication during security incident.

Adaptive and Agile Approach:

Embrace an adaptive and agile approach to cybersecurity management, recognizing that the threat landscape is constantly evolving and dynamic.

Continuously monitor and reassess the organization's risk posture, adjusting strategies, tactics, and controls in response to changing threats, technologies, and business requirements.

Foster a culture of innovation and experimentation, encouraging teams to explore new security technologies, methodologies, and approaches to address emerging threats effectively.

Embracing a Culture of Continuous Improvement

Embracing a culture of continuous improvement is essential for cybersecurity managers to adapt to evolving threats, enhance security capabilities, and foster a proactive approach to cybersecurity within their organizations. Here's how to achieve this:

Set Clear Expectations and Goals:

Define clear objectives and performance metrics related to cybersecurity, such as reducing incident response times, increasing employee awareness, or improving vulnerability management.

Communicate these goals to team members and stakeholders, emphasizing the importance of continuous improvement in achieving cybersecurity excellence.

Encourage Learning and Development:

Support ongoing learning and professional development for cybersecurity team members through training programs, certifications, workshops, and conferences. Encourage employees to pursue areas of interest and expertise within cybersecurity, fostering a culture of knowledge sharing and skill enhancement.

Promote Innovation and Creativity:

Encourage innovation and creativity in cybersecurity practices, encouraging team members to explore new technologies, methodologies, and approaches to address emerging threats.

Provide opportunities for experimentation and pilot projects, allowing team members to test and evaluate new security solutions and strategies.

Implement Feedback Mechanisms:

Establish feedback mechanisms, such as regular performance reviews, surveys, and suggestion boxes, to gather input from team members on areas for improvement.

Actively solicit feedback from stakeholders, including IT teams, business units, and executive leadership, to identify opportunities to enhance cybersecurity processes and practices.

Emphasize Collaboration and Teamwork:

Foster a collaborative and inclusive work environment where team members feel empowered to contribute their ideas, insights, and expertise.

Encourage cross-functional collaboration between cybersecurity teams and other departments, promoting alignment and integration of security efforts across the organization.

Celebrate Successes and Learn from Failures:

Recognize and celebrate achievements and milestones related to cybersecurity, such as successful implementation of new security controls or improvements in incident response capabilities.

Encourage a culture of learning from failures and mistakes, emphasizing the importance of identifying root causes, implementing corrective actions, and preventing recurrence.

Lead by Example:

Lead by example as a cybersecurity manager, demonstrating a commitment to continuous improvement through your own actions and behaviors. Show willingness to adapt and evolve in response to changing circumstances, remaining open to feedback and receptive to new ideas and perspectives.

Regularly Review and Adjust Strategies:

Regularly review cybersecurity strategies, processes, and controls to assess their effectiveness and identify areas for refinement.

Adjust strategies and priorities based on lessons learned from incidents, changes in the threat landscape, and evolving business requirements, ensuring alignment with organizational goals and objectives.

By embracing a culture of continuous improvement, cybersecurity managers can create an environment where innovation, collaboration, and adaptability thrive, enabling their teams to stay ahead of emerging threats and effectively protect the organization's assets and data.

Leading Innovation in Cyber Security Management

Leading innovation in cybersecurity management requires a proactive approach to identifying emerging threats, leveraging new technologies, and implementing cutting-edge strategies to enhance security posture. Here's an approach and overview for fostering innovation in cybersecurity management:

Stay Informed and Analyze Trends:

Keep abreast of emerging trends, technologies, and threats in the cybersecurity landscape through industry publications, research reports, and participation in professional networks and forums.

Analyze the potential impact of emerging technologies, such as AI/ML, cloud computing, IoT, and blockchain, on cybersecurity risk and resilience.

Encourage a Culture of Innovation:

Foster a culture of innovation within the cybersecurity team and across the organization, where team members are encouraged to explore new ideas, experiment with novel approaches, and challenge conventional thinking.

Create opportunities for brainstorming, idea generation, and collaborative problem-solving to spark creativity and innovation.

Promote Cross-Functional Collaboration:

Encourage collaboration and knowledge sharing between cybersecurity teams and other departments, such as IT, engineering, product development, and business units.

Establish cross-functional teams to address complex cybersecurity challenges, leveraging diverse perspectives and expertise from different areas of the organization.

Invest in Research and Development:

Allocate resources for research and development (R&D) initiatives focused on exploring innovative cybersecurity technologies, methodologies, and solutions.

Partner with academic institutions, industry consortia, and research organizations to collaborate on R&D projects and leverage external expertise.

Pilot and Test Emerging Technologies:
Identify opportunities to pilot and test emerging cybersecurity technologies and solutions in a controlled environment, such as a sandbox or lab environment.

Conduct proof-of-concept (POC) projects to evaluate the effectiveness, scalability, and usability of new security tools and technologies before full-scale deployment.

Implement Security by Design Principles:

Integrate security considerations into the design and development of new systems, applications, and technologies from the outset, following security by design principles.

Collaborate with product development teams to embed security features and controls into the software development lifecycle (SDLC), ensuring that security is an inherent part of the product architecture.

Encourage Entrepreneurial Thinking:

Encourage entrepreneurial thinking and a startup mindset among cybersecurity team members, empowering them to take risks, experiment with new approaches, and pursue innovative solutions to cybersecurity challenges.

Provide support and resources for intrapreneurial initiatives, such as innovation labs, hackathons, and incubator programs, to foster creativity and initiative.

Measure and Evaluate Impact:

Establish metrics and key performance indicators (KPIs) to measure the impact and effectiveness of innovation initiatives in improving cybersecurity outcomes.

Regularly assess the return on investment (ROI) of innovation projects, considering factors such as risk reduction, operational efficiency, and business enablement.

Adapt and Evolve:

Continuously iterate and refine innovation strategies based on feedback, lessons learned, and changes in the threat landscape and business environment.

Embrace agility and adaptability in responding to emerging threats and opportunities, adjusting priorities and approaches as needed to stay ahead of evolving cybersecurity risks.

Sudheer Kumar

Conclusion: The Cyber Security Journey Ahead

Reflecting on the Evolution of Cyber Security Management

As a cybersecurity manager, reflecting on the journey ahead involves recognizing the dynamic nature of the field and embracing the evolving challenges and opportunities that lie ahead. The evolution of cybersecurity management has been marked by rapid advancements in technology, shifting threat landscapes, and increasing complexity in the digital ecosystem. Looking forward, several key themes emerge that will shape the future of cybersecurity management:

Continuous Adaptation to Emerging Threats:

The threat landscape will continue to evolve, with cyber adversaries becoming more sophisticated and agile. As cybersecurity managers, we must remain vigilant and adapt our strategies, tools, and tactics to effectively detect, prevent, and respond to emerging threats.

Integration of Emerging Technologies:

Emerging technologies such as artificial intelligence, machine learning, cloud computing, and IoT present both opportunities and challenges for cybersecurity management. We must leverage these technologies to enhance security capabilities while also addressing new security risks and vulnerabilities that may arise.

Shift Towards a Risk-Based Approach: The traditional perimeter-based security model is no longer sufficient in today's interconnected and digital world. Cybersecurity management is shifting towards a risk-based approach, where organizations prioritize resources and investments based on the potential impact of threats to critical assets and operations.

Focus on Collaboration and Information Sharing:

Cybersecurity is a collective responsibility that requires collaboration and information sharing across organizational boundaries. As cybersecurity managers, we must foster partnerships with industry peers, government agencies, and other stakeholders to collectively address cyber threats and share best practices.

Emphasis on Cyber Resilience and Incident Response:

Building cyber resilience is becoming increasingly important as organizations face a growing number of cyber incidents and data breaches. Cybersecurity managers must focus on developing robust incident response capabilities, ensuring quick detection, containment, and recovery from cyber-attacks.

Promotion of Cybersecurity Awareness and Education:

People continue to be the weakest link in cybersecurity, with human error often contributing to security breaches. As cybersecurity managers, we must prioritize cybersecurity awareness and education initiatives to empower employees, partners, and customers to become more security-conscious and resilient.

Alignment with Business Objectives and Compliance Requirements:

Cybersecurity management must be closely aligned with the organization's overall business objectives and compliance requirements. Cybersecurity managers must demonstrate the value of cybersecurity investments in terms of risk reduction, operational efficiency, and regulatory compliance.

In conclusion, the journey ahead in cybersecurity management is marked by uncertainty and complexity, but also by opportunities for innovation, collaboration, and resilience. By embracing these challenges and staying ahead of emerging trends, cybersecurity managers can help their organizations navigate the evolving threat landscape and protect against cyber threats effectively.

Empowering Cyber Security Managers to Lead with Confidence

Empowering cybersecurity managers to lead with confidence involves providing them with the necessary support, resources, and opportunities to develop their skills, make informed decisions, and drive positive outcomes in their roles. Here are some strategies to empower cybersecurity managers:

Invest in Training and Development:
Provide ongoing training and professional development opportunities for cybersecurity managers to enhance their technical expertise, leadership skills, and industry knowledge.

Offer certifications, workshops, seminars, and mentoring programs to support their career growth and advancement.

Foster a Culture of Trust and Support:
Create a supportive and inclusive work environment where cybersecurity managers feel valued, respected, and empowered to voice their opinions, ideas, and concerns.

Encourage open communication, collaboration, and teamwork, fostering a sense of belonging and camaraderie among cybersecurity professionals.

Provide Clear Goals and Expectations: Set clear goals, objectives, and performance expectations for cybersecurity managers, aligning them with organizational priorities, values, and strategic initiatives.

Provide regular feedback, coaching, and recognition to acknowledge their contributions and achievements, reinforcing a sense of purpose and motivation.

Equip Them with Resources and Tools:

Ensure that cybersecurity managers have access to the resources, tools, and technologies needed to perform their roles effectively, including cybersecurity frameworks, software solutions, and threat intelligence platforms.

Invest in infrastructure, staffing, and budgetary allocations to support cybersecurity initiatives and projects, empowering managers to address security challenges proactively.

Encourage Decision-Making and Autonomy:

Empower cybersecurity managers to make informed decisions and take ownership of cybersecurity initiatives, providing them with autonomy and accountability to lead their teams effectively.

Delegate authority and responsibility appropriately, allowing managers to exercise judgment and discretion in managing risks and implementing security controls.

Promote Thought Leadership and Innovation:

Encourage cybersecurity managers to think strategically and innovatively about cybersecurity challenges and opportunities, fostering a culture of creativity, experimentation, and continuous improvement.

Recognize and celebrate innovative ideas, solutions, and initiatives that contribute to advancing cybersecurity objectives and addressing emerging threats.

Provide Opportunities for Leadership Development:

Offer leadership development programs, workshops, and coaching sessions to help cybersecurity managers enhance their leadership skills, emotional intelligence, and decision-making capabilities.

Encourage them to take on leadership roles in industry associations, professional networks, and community outreach programs, expanding their influence and visibility in the cybersecurity community.

Support Work-Life Balance and Wellbeing:

Recognize the importance of work-life balance and employee wellbeing in promoting job satisfaction, productivity, and resilience.

Provide flexible work arrangements, wellness programs, and mental health resources to support the holistic wellbeing of cybersecurity managers and their teams.

By implementing these strategies, organizations can empower cybersecurity managers to lead with confidence, enabling them to navigate the complexities of the cybersecurity landscape effectively and drive positive outcomes for their teams and organizations.

Embracing the Opportunities and Challenges of Securing the Digital Frontier

Embracing the opportunities and challenges of securing the digital frontier as a cybersecurity manager requires a proactive and strategic approach. Here's how you can effectively navigate this landscape:

Stay Informed and Educated: Continuously educate yourself about emerging technologies, threat landscapes, and cybersecurity trends. Stay updated on industry best practices, standards, and regulations to effectively address evolving challenges.

Foster a Culture of Innovation: Encourage innovation within your cybersecurity team by promoting creativity, experimentation, and out-of-the-box thinking. Explore new technologies and approaches to enhance security capabilities and stay ahead of emerging threats.

Build Strategic Partnerships: Collaborate with internal stakeholders, such as IT teams, business units, and executive leadership, to align cybersecurity initiatives with organizational goals and priorities. Establish partnerships with external entities, including industry peers, government agencies, and cybersecurity communities, to share insights and best practices.

Develop Strong Leadership Skills: Cultivate leadership qualities such as integrity, resilience, and adaptability to inspire confidence and trust among your team members and stakeholders.

Prioritize Risk Management: Adopt a risk-based approach to cybersecurity management, focusing on identifying and mitigating risks that pose the greatest threat to your organization's critical assets and operations. Implement robust risk assessment methodologies and decision-making frameworks to prioritize resource allocation and investment.

Enhance Incident Response Capabilities: Strengthen your organization's incident response capabilities to effectively detect, respond to, and recover from cyber incidents. Develop comprehensive incident response plans, conduct regular tabletop exercises and simulations, and establish clear roles and responsibilities to ensure a coordinated and effective response.

Promote Cybersecurity Awareness:

Raise awareness about cybersecurity risks and best practices among employees, partners, and customers to foster a culture of security awareness and accountability. Provide regular training and education programs, communicate security policies and guidelines, and encourage reporting of suspicious activities or incidents.

Embrace Continuous Improvement:

Embrace a mindset of continuous improvement, seeking opportunities to enhance cybersecurity processes, technologies, and practices. Regularly assess and evaluate your organization's security posture, learn from past experiences and industry insights, and adapt your strategies accordingly to stay agile and resilient in the face of evolving threats.

By embracing these strategies, cybersecurity managers can effectively navigate the opportunities and challenges of securing the digital frontier, empowering their organizations to mitigate risks, protect critical assets, and achieve cybersecurity excellence.

Appendix: Resources for Cyber Security Managers

Recommended Reading List

Here is a recommended top 10 online reading list for cyber security managers:

Krebs on Security (https://krebsonsecurity.com):

Run by investigative journalist Brian Krebs, this blog provides in-depth analysis of cyber security news, trends, and breaches, offering valuable insights into the evolving threat landscape.

Schneier on Security (https://www.schneier.com):

Bruce Schneier, a renowned security expert, shares his thoughts on security topics ranging from cryptography to privacy, offering insightful commentary and analysis.

Dark Reading (https://www.darkreading.com):

Dark Reading is a leading cybersecurity news website that covers a wide range of topics, including threat intelligence, vulnerability management, and incident response.

Cyber Security Manager's Handbook

The Hacker News (https://thehackernews.com):

This popular cybersecurity news portal provides up-to-date coverage of hacking incidents, vulnerabilities, and security research, keeping readers informed about the latest threats and trends.

SANS Internet Storm Center (https://isc.sans.edu):

Operated by the SANS Institute, the Internet Storm Center offers daily analysis and commentary on cybersecurity threats and incidents, providing valuable insights for security professionals.

SecurityWeek: (https://www.securityweek.com):

SecurityWeek covers cybersecurity news, analysis, and insights, with a focus on industry trends, technology developments, and best practices.

InfoSec Resources (https://resources.infosecinstitute.com):

InfoSec Resources offers a wealth of articles, tutorials, and guides on a wide range of cybersecurity topics, including ethical hacking, incident response, and compliance.

Cybrary (https://www.cybrary.it):

Cybrary offers a variety of free and paid courses, webinars, and resources for cybersecurity professionals, covering topics such as penetration testing, digital forensics, and security certifications.

NIST Cybersecurity Framework:

(https://www.nist.gov/cyberframework): The National Institute of Standards and Technology (NIST) Cybersecurity Framework provides guidance for organizations to manage and reduce cybersecurity risk, offering a comprehensive set of resources and best practices.

OWASP (https://owasp.org):

The Open Web Application Security Project (OWASP) is a community-driven organization that provides resources and tools for improving the security of web applications, including guides, cheat sheets, and vulnerability databases.

These online resources cover a wide range of cybersecurity topics and provide valuable insights, news, and educational materials for cyber security managers looking to stay informed and enhance their skills in the field

Online Training and Certification Programs

These are the list of online training and certification programs suitable for cyber security managers:

Certified Information Systems Security Professional (CISSP): Offered by (ISC)², the CISSP certification is a globally recognized credential for experienced cyber security professionals. It covers a broad range of security topics, including security and risk management, asset security, and security operations.

Certified Information Security Manager (CISM): Offered by ISACA, the CISM certification is designed for individuals responsible for managing, designing, and overseeing an enterprise's information security program. It focuses on governance, risk management, and incident response.

Certified Information Security Auditor (CISA): Also offered by ISACA, the CISA certification is ideal for professionals involved in auditing, control, and assurance of information systems. It covers auditing processes, governance, and IT management.

Certified Cloud Security Professional (CCSP): Offered by (ISC)², the CCSP certification is designed for IT and information security leaders who are responsible for managing and securing cloud environments. It covers cloud security architecture, design, operations, and compliance.

CompTIA Security+: The CompTIA Security+ certification is an entry-level certification that validates foundational cybersecurity skills and knowledge. It covers topics such as threat management, cryptography, and network security.

Certified Ethical Hacker (CEH): Offered by the EC-Council, the CEH certification is for professionals who want to demonstrate their understanding of ethical hacking and penetration testing techniques. It covers topics such as reconnaissance, scanning, and enumeration.

Certified Information Security Management Principles (CISMP): Offered by the British Computer Society (BCS), the CISMP certification is ideal for individuals involved in information security management roles. It covers information security governance, risk management, and compliance.

GIAC Security Leadership (GSLC): Offered by the Global Information Assurance Certification (GIAC), the GSLC certification is designed for professionals responsible for leading cybersecurity teams and managing security programs. It covers leadership, risk management, and security policy development.

Certified Cyber Security Management Professional (CCSMP): Offered by the Certified Information Security, the CCSMP certification is tailored for cyber security managers and focuses on strategic planning, risk management, and leadership skills.

Cybersecurity Nexus (CSX) Certifications: Offered by ISACA, the CSX certification program includes multiple certifications focused on different aspects of cybersecurity, including cyber security fundamentals, cyber security operations, and cyber security leadership.

These certification programs provide valuable knowledge, skills, and credentials for cyber security managers looking to enhance their expertise and advance their careers in the field. It's essential to research each certification program to determine which best aligns with your career goals and professional development needs.

Professional Organizations and Networking Opportunities

These are some professional organizations and networking opportunities for cyber security managers:

(ISC)² (International Information System Security Certification Consortium): (ISC)² offers networking opportunities, professional development resources, and certifications such as CISSP (Certified Information Systems Security Professional) and CCSP (Certified Cloud Security Professional).

ISACA (Information Systems Audit and Control Association): ISACA provides networking events, conferences, and certifications such as CISM (Certified Information Security Manager) and CISA (Certified Information Systems Auditor).

ISSA (Information Systems Security Association): ISSA is a global organization that offers networking events, webinars, and local chapter meetings for cyber security professionals.

(ISC)² Chapter Meetings: (ISC)² chapters host regular meetings, seminars, and workshops for cyber security professionals to network, share knowledge, and earn continuing education credits.

OWASP (Open Web Application Security Project): OWASP is a global community dedicated to improving the security of software. It offers local chapter meetings, conferences, and online resources for cyber security professionals focused on application security.

Cloud Security Alliance (CSA): CSA provides networking opportunities, research reports, and educational resources focused on cloud security. It hosts events such as the CSA Summit and offers certifications like the CCSK (Certificate of Cloud Security Knowledge).

InfraGard: InfraGard is a partnership between the FBI and the private sector that provides networking opportunities, information sharing, and training related to critical infrastructure protection and cyber security.

Information Security Forum (ISF): ISF is a global organization that provides networking events, research reports, and best practice guides for cyber security professionals in large organizations.

Local Cyber Security Meetup Groups: Many cities have local cyber security meetup groups where professionals can network, share knowledge, and collaborate on projects. Websites like Meetup.com can help you find local groups in your area.

Cyber Security Conferences:

Attend cyber security conferences such as RSA Conference, Black Hat, DEF CON, and SecureWorld to network with industry peers, learn about the latest trends, and participate in hands-on training sessions.

These organizations and networking opportunities provide valuable resources for cyber security managers to stay informed, connect with peers, and advance their careers in the field

About the Author

Sudheer Kumar is a seasoned cybersecurity professional with over 15 years of experience in the field of Networking and Cyber Security. With a passion for technology and a deep understanding of digital threats, Sudheer Kumar has dedicated their career to helping organizations protect their sensitive information and safeguard against cyberattacks.

Sudheer Kumar holds a Master Degree in Electronics and Communication with specialized in Embedded System. They have worked in various roles within the MNC's and startups (Fintech, Manufacturing, IT, Telecom) industry where they gained hands-on experience in Cyber-Resilience strategy, SOC Management, incident response, vulnerability assessment, and security architecture design.

Throughout their career, **Sudheer Kumar** has remained at the forefront of cybersecurity trends, continuously adapting to the evolving threat landscape, and mastering the latest tools and techniques. They are known for their expertise in IT Security, Cybersecurity, Cyber-Resilience strategy and have delivered numerous presentations and workshops on the topic at industry conferences and events.

In addition to their professional work, **Sudheer Kumar** is passionate about education and knowledge sharing. They regularly contribute articles and insights to cybersecurity publications and online forums, aiming to empower others with the knowledge and skills needed to protect themselves in an increasingly digital world.

Sudheer Kumar commitment to excellence and their contributions to the cybersecurity community have earned them recognition and accolades from peers and industry experts alike. They are honored to share their expertise in this book and hope that it will serve as a valuable resource for readers seeking to enhance their understanding of as a cybersecurity manager and mitigate digital risks effectively.

Connect with Sudheer Kumar:

LinkedIn: https://www.linkedin.com/in/sudheer-kumar-841a4244/
Email: sudheedhukya1990@gmail.com

www.ingramcontent.com/pod-product-compliance
Lightning Source LLC
Chambersburg PA
CBHW052207220526
45471CB00004B/1851